CHAPTER I
HISTORICAL

The position of women in social life was for a long time a matter of course. It did not arise as a question, because it was taken for granted. The dominance of men seemed to derive so obviously from natural causes, from the possession of faculties physical, moral and intellectual, in men, which were wanting in women, that no one thought of questioning the situation. At the same time, the inferiority of woman was never conceived as so great as to diminish seriously, much less to eliminate altogether, her responsibility for crimes she might commit. There were cases, of course, such as that of offences committed by women under coverture, in which a diminution of responsibility was recognised and was given effect to in condonation of the offence and in mitigation of the punishment. But there was no sentiment in general in favour of a female more than of a male criminal. It entered into the head of no one to weep tears of pity over the murderess of a lover or husband rather than over the murderer of a sweetheart or wife. Similarly, minor offenders, a female blackmailer, a female thief, a female perpetrator of an assault, was not deemed less guilty or worthy of more lenient treatment than a male offender in like cases. The law, it was assumed, and the assumption was acted upon, was the same for both sexes. The sexes were equal before the law. The laws were harsher in some respects than now, although not perhaps in all. But there was no special line of demarcation as regards the punishment of offences as between men and women. The penalty ordained by the law for crime or misdemeanour was the same for both and in general applied equally to both. Likewise in civil suits, proceedings were not specially weighted against the man and in favour of the woman. There was, as a general rule, no very noticeable sex partiality in the administration of the law.

This state of affairs continued in England till well into the nineteenth century. Thenceforward a change began to take place. Modern Feminism rose slowly above the horizon. Modern Feminism has two distinct sides to it: (1) an articulate political and economic side embracing demands for so-called rights; and (2) a sentimental side which insists in an accentuation of the privileges and immunities which have grown up, not articulately or as the result of definite demands, but as the consequence of sentimental pleading in particular cases. In this way, however, a public opinion became established, finding expression in a sex favouritism in the law and even still more in its administration, in favour of women as against men.

These two sides of Modern Feminism are not necessarily combined in the same person. One may, for example, find opponents of female suffrage who are strong advocates of sentimental favouritism towards women in matters of law and its administration. On the other hand you may find, though this is more rare, strong advocates of political and other rights for the female sex, who sincerely deprecate the present inequality of the law in favour of women. As a rule, however, the two sides go together, the vast bulk of the advocates of "Women's Rights" being equally keen on the retention and extension of women's privileges. Indeed, it would seem as though the main object of the bulk of the advocates of the "Woman's Movement" was to convert the female sex into the position of a dominant *sexe noblesse*. The two sides of Feminism have advanced hand in hand for the last two generations, though it was the purely sentimental side that first appeared as a factor in public opinion.

The attempt to paint women in a different light to the traditional one of physical, intellectual and moral inferiority to men, probably received its first literary expression in a treatise published in 1532 by Cornelius Agrippa of Nettesheim entitled *De Nobilitate et Praecellentia Feminei Sexus* and dedicated to Margaret, Regent of the Netherlands, whose favour Agrippa was at that time desirous of courting. The ancient world has nothing to offer in the shape of literary forerunners of Modern Feminism, although that industrious collector of historical odds and ends, Valerius Maximus, relates the story of one Afrania who, with some of her friends, created disturbances in the Law Courts of ancient Rome in her attempt to make women's voices heard before the tribunals. As regards more recent ages, after Agrippa, we have to wait till the early years of the eighteenth century for another instance of Feminism before its time, in an essay on the subject of woman by Daniel Defoe. But it was not till the closing years of the eighteenth century that any considerable expression of opinion in favour of changing the relative positions of the sexes, by upsetting the view of their respective values, founded on the general experience of mankind, made itself noticeable.

The names of Mary Wollstonecraft in English literature and of Condorcet in French, will hardly fail to occur to the reader in this connection. During the French Revolution the crazy Olympe de Gouges achieved ephemeral notoriety by her claim for the intellectual equality of women with men.

Up to this time (the close of the eighteenth century) no advance whatever had been made by legislation in recognising the modern theory of sex equality. The claims of women and their apologists for entering upon the functions of men, political, social or otherwise, although put forward from time to time by isolated individuals, received little countenance from public opinion, and still less from the law. What I have called, however, the sentimental aspect of Modern Feminism undoubtedly did make some headway in public opinion by the end of the eighteenth century, and grew in volume during the early years of the nineteenth century. It effectuated in the Act passed in 1820 by the English Parliament abolishing the punishment of flogging for female criminals. This was the first beginning of the differentiation of the sexes in the matter of the criminal law. The parliamentary debate on the Bill in question shows clearly enough the power that Sentimental[15:1] Feminism had acquired in public opinion in the course of a generation, for no proposal was made at the same time to abolish the punishment of flogging so far as men were concerned. Up to this time the criminal law of England, as of other countries, made no distinction whatever between the sexes in the matter of crime and punishment, or at least no distinction based on the principle or sentiment of sex privilege. (A slight exception might be made, perhaps, in the crime of "petty treason," which distinguished the murder of a husband by his wife from other cases of homicide.) But from this time forward, legislation and administration have diverged farther and farther from the principle of sex equality in this connection in favour of female immunity, the result being that at the present day, assuming the punishment meted out to the woman for a given crime to represent a normal penalty, the man receives an additional increment over and above that accorded to the crime, *for the offenceofhavingbeenbornamanandnotawoman*   .

I should explain that I attach a distinct meaning to the word *sentimental*; as used by me it does not signify, as it does with most people, an excess of sentiment over and above what I feel myself, but a sentiment unequally distributed. As used in this sense, the repulsion to the flogging of women while no repulsion is felt to the flogging of men is *sentimentalism* pure and simple. On the other hand the objection to flogging altogether as punishment for men or women could not be described as sentimentalism, whatever else it might be. In the same way the anti-vivisectionist's aversion to "physiological" experiments on animals, if confined to household pets and not extended to other animals, might be justly described as sentimentalism; but one who objected to such experiments on all animals, no matter whether one agreed with his point of view or not, could not be justly charged with sentimentalism (or at least, not unless, while objecting to vivisection, he or she were prepared to condone other acts involving an equal amount of cruelty to animals).

The Original Divorce Law of 1857 in its provisions respecting costs and alimony, constitutes another landmark in the matter of female privilege before the law. Other measures of unilateral sex legislation followed in the years ensuing until the present state of things, by which the whole power of the State is practically at the disposal of woman to coerce and oppress men. But this side of the question we propose to deal with later on.

The present actual movement of Feminism in political and social life may be deemed to have begun in the early sixties, in the agitation which preceded the motion of John Stuart Mill in 1867, on the question of conferring the parliamentary franchise upon women. This was coincident with an agitation for the opening of various careers to women, notably the medical faculty. We are speaking, of course, here of Great Britain, which was first in the field in Europe, alike in the theory and practice of Modern Feminism. But the publication by the great protagonist of the movement, John Stuart Mill, of his book, "The Subjection of Women," in 1868, endowed the cause with a literary gospel which was soon translated into the chief languages of the Continent, and corresponding movements started in other countries. Strangely enough, it made considerable headway in Russia, the awakening of Russia to Western ideas having recently begun to make itself felt at the time of which we are speaking. The movement henceforth took its place as a permanent factor in the political and social life of this and other countries. Bills for female suffrage were introduced every year into the British House of Commons with, on the whole, yearly diminishing majorities against these measures, till a few years back the scale turned on the other side, and the Women's Enfranchisement Bill passed every year its second reading until 1912, when for the first time for many years it was rejected by a small majority. Meanwhile both sides of the Feminist movement, apart from the question of the franchise, had been gaining in influence. Municipal franchise "on the same terms as for men" had been conceded. Women have voted for and sat on School Boards, Boards of Guardians, and other public bodies. Their claim to exercise the medical profession has been not merely admitted in law but recognised in public opinion for long past. All the advantages of an academic career have been opened to them, with the solitary exception of the actual conferment of degrees at Oxford and Cambridge. Such has been the growth of the articulate and political side of the theory of Modern Feminism.

The sentimental side of Feminism, with its practical result of the overweighting of justice in the interests of women in the courts, civil as well as criminal, and their practical immunity from the operation of the criminal law when in the dock, has advanced correspondingly; while at the same time the sword of that same criminal law is sharpened to a razor edge against the man even accused, let alone convicted, of any offence against the sacrosanct majesty of "Womanhood." Such is the present position of the Woman question in this country, which we take as typical, in the sense that in Great Britain, to which we may also add the United States of America and the British Colonies, where—if possible, the movement is stronger than in the mother country itself—we see the logical outcome of Feminist theory and sentiment. It remains to consider the existing facts more in detail, and the psychological bearings of that large number of persons who have been in the recent past, and are being at the present time, influenced to accept the dogmas of Modern Feminism and the statements of alleged facts made by its votaries. Before doing so it behoves us to examine the credibility of the dogmas themselves, and the nature of the arguments used to support them and also the accuracy of the alleged facts employed by the Feminists to stimulate the indignation of the popular mind against the pretended wrongs of women.

CHAPTER II
THE MAIN DOGMA OF MODERN FEMINISM

We have pointed out in the last chapter that Modern Feminism has two sides, the positive, definite, and articulate side, which ostensibly claims equality between the sexes, the chief concern of which is the conferring of all the rights and duties of men upon women, and the opening up of all careers to them. The justification of these demands is based upon the dogma, that, notwithstanding appearances to the contrary, women are endowed by nature with the same capacity intellectually and morally as men. We have further pointed out that there is another side in Modern Feminism which in a vague way claims for women immunity from criminal law and special privileges on the ground of sex in civil law. The basis of this side of Feminism is a sentimentalism—*i.e.* an unequally distributed sentiment in favour of women, traditional and acquired. It is seldom even attempted to base this sentimental claim for women on argument at all. The utmost attempts in this direction amount to vague references to physical weakness, and to the claim for special consideration deriving from the old theory of the mental and moral weakness of the female sex, so strenuously combated as out of date, when the first side of Modern Feminism is being contended for. The more or less inchoate assumptions of the second or sentimental side of the modern "Woman's Movement" amounts practically, as already stated, to a claim for women to be allowed to commit crimes without incurring the penalties imposed by the law for similar crimes when committed by men. It should be noted that in practice the most strenuous advocates of the positive and articulate side of Feminism are also the sincerest upholders of the unsubstantial and inarticulate assumptions of the sentimental side of the same creed. This is noticeable whenever a woman is found guilty of a particularly atrocious crime. It is somewhat rare for women to be convicted of such crimes at all, since the influence of sentimental Feminism with judges and juries is sufficient to procure an acquittal, no matter how conclusive the evidence to the contrary. Even if women are found guilty it is usual for a virtually nominal sentence to be passed. Should, however, a woman by any chance be convicted of a heinous crime, such as murder or maiming, under specially aggravated circumstances, and a sentence be passed such as would be unanimously sanctioned by public opinion in the case of a man, then we find the whole Feminist world up in arms. The outcry is led by self-styled upholders of equality between the sexes, the apostles of the positive side of Feminism, who *bien entendu* claim the eradication of sex boundaries in political and social life on the ground of women being of equal capacity with men, but who, when moral responsibility is in question, conveniently fall back on a sentiment, the only conceivable ground for which is to be found in the time-honoured theory of the mental and moral weakness of the female sex. As illustrations of the truth of the foregoing, the reader may be referred to the cases of Florence Doughty in 1906, who shot at and wounded a solicitor with whom she had relations, together with his son; to Daisy Lord in 1908, for the murder of her new-born child; to the case of the Italian murderess, Napolitano in Canada, convicted of the cold-blooded butchery of her husband in his sleep in 1911, for whose reprieve a successful agitation was got up by the suffrage societies!

Let us first of all consider the dogma at the basis of the positive side of Modern Feminism, which claims rational grounds of fact and reason for itself, and professes to be able to make good its case by virtue of such grounds. This dogma consists in the assertion of equality in intellectual capacity, in spite of appearances to the contrary, of women with men. I think it will be admitted that the articulate objects of Modern Feminism, taking them one with another, rest on this dogma, and on this dogma alone. I know it has been argued as regards the question of suffrage, that the demand does not rest solely upon the admission of equality of capacity, since men of a notoriously inferior mental order are not excluded from voting upon that ground, but the fallacy of this last argument is obvious. In all these matters we have to deal with averages. Public opinion has hitherto recognised the average of women as being intellectually below the voting standard, and the average man as not. This, if admitted, is enough to establish the anti-suffrage thesis. The latter is not affected by the fact that it is possible to find certain individual men of inferior intelligence and therefore less intrinsically qualified to form a political judgment than certain specially gifted women. The pretended absurdity of "George Eliot having no vote, and of her gardener having one" is really no absurdity at all. In the first place, given the economic advantages which conferred education upon the novelist, and not upon the gardener, there is not sufficient evidence available that his judgment in public affairs might not have been even superior to that of George Eliot herself. Moreover, the possession of exceptionally strong imaginative faculty, expressing itself as literary genius or talent in works of fiction, does not necessarily imply exceptional power of political judgment. But, be this as it may, where averages are in question, exceptions obviously do not count.

The underlying assumption of the suffrage movement may therefore be taken to be the average equality of the sexes as regards intellectual value. [24:1]

[24:1] I believe there are some Feminist fanatics who pretend to maintain the superiority of the female mind, but I doubt whether this thesis is taken seriously even by those who put it forward. In any case there are limits to the patent absurditie which it is worth while to refute by argument.

An initial difficulty exists in proving theoretically the intellectual inferiority of women to men, or even their relative unsuitability for fulfilling functions involving a special order of judgment. There are such things as matters of fact which are open to common observation and which none think of denying or calling in question unless they have some special reason for doing so. Now it is always possible to deny a fact, however evident it may be to ordinary perception, and it is equally impossible to prove that the person calling in question the aforesaid evident fact is either lying (or shall we say is "prevaricating"), or even that he is a person hopelessly abnormal in his organs of sense-perception.

At the time of writing, the normal person who has no axe to grind in maintaining the contrary, declares the sun to be shining brightly, but should it answer the purpose of anyone to deny this obvious fact, and declare that the day is gloomy and overcast, there is no power of argument by which I can prove that I am right and he is wrong. I may point to the sun, but if he chooses to affirm that he doesn't see it I can't prove that he does. This is, of course, an extreme case, scarcely likely to occur in actual life. But it is in essence similar to those cases of persons (and they are not seldom met with) who, when they find facts hopelessly destructive of a certain theoretical position adopted by them, do not hesitate to cut the knot of controversy in their own favour by boldly denying the inconvenient facts. One often has experience of this trick of controversy in discussing the question of the notorious characteristics of the female sex. The Feminist driven into a corner endeavours to save his face by flatly denying matters open to common observation and admitted as obvious by all who are not Feminists. Such facts are the pathological mental condition peculiar to the female sex, commonly connoted by the term hysteria; the absence, or at best the extremely imperfect development of the logical faculty in most women; the inability of the average woman in her judgment of things to rise above personal considerations; and, what is largely a consequence of this, the lack of a sense of abstract justice and fair play among women in general. The aforesaid peculiarities of women, as women, are, I contend, matters of common observation and are only disputed by those persons—to wit Feminists—to whose theoretical views and practical demands their admission would be inconvenient if not fatal. Of course these characterisations refer to averages, and they do not exclude partial or even occasionally striking exceptions. It is possible, therefore, although perhaps not very probable, that individual experience may in the case of certain individuals play a part in falsifying their general outlook; it is possible— although, as I before said not perhaps very probable—that any given man's experience of the other sex has been limited to a few quite exceptional women and that hence his particular experience contradicts that of the general run of mankind. In this case, of course, his refusal to admit what to others are self-evident facts would be perfectly *bona fide*. The above highly improbable contingency is the only refuge for those who would contend for sincerity in the Feminist's denials. In this matter I only deal with the male Feminist. The female Feminist is usually too biassed a witness in this particular question.

Now let us consider the whole of the differentiations of the mental character between man and woman in the light of a further generalisation which is sufficiently obvious in itself and which has been formulated with special clearness by the late Otto Weininger in his remarkable book, "Geschlecht und Charakter" (Sex and Character). I refer to the observations contained in Section II., Chaps. 2 and 3. The point has been, of course, previously noted, and the present writer, among others, has on various occasions called special attention to it. But its formulation and elaboration by Weininger is the most complete I know. The truth in question consists in the fact, undeniable to all those not rendered impervious to facts by preconceived dogma, that, as I have elsewhere put it, while man *has* a sex, woman *is* a sex. Let us hear Weininger on this point. "Woman is *only* sexual, man is *also* sexual. Alike in time and space this difference may be traced in man, parts of his body susceptible to sexual excitement are small in number and strictly localised. In woman sexuality is diffused over the whole body, every contact on whatever part excites her sexually." Weininger points out that while the sexual element in man, owing to the physiological character of the sexual organs, may be at times more violent than that in woman, yet that it is spasmodic and occurs in crises separated by intervals of quiescence. In woman, on the other hand, while less spasmodic, it is continuous. The sexual instinct with man being, as he styles it, "an appendix" and no more, he can raise himself mentally entirely outside of it. "He is conscious of it as of something which he possesses but which is not inseparate from the rest of his nature. He can view it objectively. With woman this is not the case; the sex element is part of her whole nature. Hence, it is not as with man, clearly recognisable in local manifestations, but subtly affects the whole life of the organism. For this reason the man is conscious of the sexual element within him as such, whereas the woman is unconscious of it as such. It is not for nothing that in common parlance woman is spoken of as 'the sex.' In this sexual differentiation of the whole life-nature of woman from man, deducible as it is from physiological and anatomical distinctions, lies the ground of those differentiations of function which culminate in the fact that while mankind in its intellectual, moral and technical development is represented in the main by Man, Woman has continued to find her chief function in the direct procreation of the race." A variety of causes, notably modern economic development, in their effect on family life, also the illegitimate application of the modern democratic notion of the equality of classes and races, to that of sex, has contributed to the modern revolt against natural sex limitations.

Assuming the substantial accuracy of the above statement of fact, the absurdity and cheapness of the clap-trap of the modern "social purity" monger, as to having one and the same sexual morality for both sexes will be readily seen. The recognition of the necessity of admitting greater latitude in this respect to men than to women is based clearly on physiology and common-sense. With men sexual instinct manifests itself locally, and at intervals its satisfaction is an urgent and pressing need. With woman this is not so. Hence the recognised distinction between the sexes in this respect is, as far as it goes, a thoroughly sound one. Not that I am championing the severity of the restrictions of the current sexual code as regards women. On the contrary, I think it ought to be and will be, in a reasonable society of the future, considerably relaxed. I am only pointing out that the urgency is not so great in the one case as in the other. And this fact it is which has led to the toleration of a stringency, originally arising mainly from economic causes (questions of inheritance and the like), in the case of women, which would not have been tolerated in that of men, even had similar reasons for its adoption in their case obtained. Any successful attempt of social purity mongers to run counter to physiology in enforcing either by legislation or public opinion the same stringency on men in this respect as on women could but have the most disastrous consequences to the health and well-being of the community.

It was a saying of the late Dr Henry Maudsley: *"Sex lies deeper than culture."* By this we may understand to be meant that sex differences are organic. All authorities on the physiological question are agreed that woman is less well-organised, less well-developed, than man. Dr de Varigny asserts that this fact is traceable throughout the whole female organism, throughout all its tissues, and all its functions. For instance, the stature of the human female is less than that of the man in all races. As regards weight there is a corresponding difference. The adult woman weighs, on the average, rather more than 11 lbs. less than the man; moreover as a rule a woman completes her growth some years earlier than a man. The bones are lighter in the woman than in the man; not absolutely but in proportion to the weight of the body. They are, it is stated, not merely thinner but more fragile. The difference may be traced even to their chemical composition. The whole muscular development is inferior in woman to that in man by about one-third. The heart in woman is smaller and lighter than in man—being about 10½ oz. in man as against slightly over 8 oz. in woman. In the woman the respiratory organs show less chest and lung capacity. Again, the blood contains a considerably less proportion of red to white corpuscles. Finally, we come to the question of the size and constitution of the brain. (It should be observed that all these distinctions of sex show themselves more or less from birth onwards.)

Specialists are agreed that at all ages the size of the brain of woman is less than that of man. The difference in relative size is greater in proportion according to the degree of civilisation. This is noteworthy, as it would seem as though the brain of man grew with the progress of civilisation, whereas that of woman remains nearly stationary. The average proportion as regards size of skull between the woman and man of to-day is as 85 to 100. The weight of brain in woman varies from 38½ oz. to 45½ oz.; in man, from 42 oz. to 49 oz. This represents the absolute difference in weight, but, according to Dr de Varigny, the relative weight—*i.e.* the weight in proportion to that of the whole body—is even more striking in its indication of inferiority. The weight of the brain in woman is but one-forty-fourth of the weight of the body, while in man it is one-fortieth. This difference accentuates itself with age. It is only 7 per cent. in favour of man between twenty and thirty years; it is 11 per cent. between thirty and forty years. As regards the substance of the brain itself and its convolutions, the enormous majority of physiologists are practically unanimous in declaring that the female brain is simpler and smoother, its convolutions fewer and more superficial than those of the male brain, that the frontal lobes, generally associated with the intellectual faculties, are less developed than the occipital lobes, which are universally connected with the lower psychological functions. The grey substance is poorer and less abundant in woman than in man, while the blood vessels of the occipital region are correspondingly fuller than those supplying the frontal lobes. In man the case is exactly the reverse. It cannot be denied by any sane person familiar with the barest elements of physiology that the whole female organism is subservient to the functions of child-bearing and lactation, which explains the inferior development of those organs and faculties which are not specially connected with this supreme end of Woman.

It is the fashion of Feminists, ignoring these fundamental physiological sex differences, to affirm that the actual inferiority of women, where they have the honesty to admit such an obvious fact, is accountable by the centuries of oppression in which Woman has been held by wicked and evil-minded Man. The absurdity of this contention has been more than once pointed out. Assuming its foundation in fact, what does it imply? Clearly that the girls inherit only through their mothers and boys only through their fathers, an hypothesis plainly at variance with the known facts of heredity.

Yet those who maintain that distinction of intelligence, etc., between the sexes are traceable to external conditions affecting one sex only and inherited through that sex alone, cannot evade the above assumption. Those, therefore, who regard it as an article of their faith that Woman would show herself not inferior in mental power to man, if only she had the chance of exercising that power, must find a surer foundation for their opinion than this theory of the centuries of oppression, under which, as they allege, the female sex has laboured.

We now come to the important question of morbid and pathological mental conditions to which the female sex is liable and which are usually connected with those constitutional disturbances of the nervous system which pass under the name of *hysteria*. The word is, as everyone knows, derived from *hystera—the womb*, and was uniformly regarded by the ancients as directly due to disease of the *uterus*, this view maintaining itself in modern medicine up till well-nigh the middle of the nineteenth century. Thus Dr J. Mason Good (in his "Study of Medicine," 1822, vol. iii., p. 528, an important medical text-book during the earlier half of the nineteenth century) says: "With a morbid condition of this organ, hysteria is in many instances very closely connected, though it is going too far to say that it is always dependent upon such condition, for we meet with instances, occasionally, in which no possible connexion can be traced between the disease and the organ," etc. This is perhaps the first appearance, certainly in English medicine, of doubts being thrown on the uterine origin of the various symptoms grouped under the general term, *hysteria*. Towards the latter part of the nineteenth century the prevalent view tended more and more to dissociate hysteria from uterine trouble. Lately, however, some eminent pathologists have shown a tendency to qualify the terms of the latter view. Thus Dr Thomas Stevenson in 1902 admits that "it [hysteria] frequently accompanies a morbid state of the uterus," especially where inflammation and congestion are present, and it is not an uncommon thing for surgeons at the present time to remove the ovaries in obstinate cases of hysteria. On the other hand Dr Thomas Buzzard, in an article on the subject in Quain's *Dictionary of Medicine*, 1902, states that hysteria is only exceptionally found in women suffering from diseases of the genital organs, and its relation to uterine and ovarian disturbances is probably neither more nor less than that which pertains to the other affections of the nervous system which may occur without any obvious material cause. Dr Thomas Luff ("Text-Book on Forensic Medicine," 1895) shows that the derangements of the reproductive functions are undoubtedly the cause of various attacks of insanity in the female. Dr Savage, in his book "On Neuroses," says that acute mania in women occurs most frequently at the period of adult and mature life, and may occasionally take place at either extreme age. Acute mania sometimes occurs at the suppression of the *menses*. The same is true of melancholia and other pathological mental symptoms. Dr Luff states that acute mania may replace hysteria; that this happens at periods such as puberty, change of life and menstruation. These patients in the intervals of their attacks are often morbidly irritable or excitable, but as time goes on their energies become diminished and their emotions blunted ("Forensic Medicine," ii. 307). Such patients are often seized with a desire to commit violence; they are often very mischievous, tearing up clothes, breaking windows, etc. In this mental disorder the patient is driven by a morbid and uncontrollable impulse to such acts. It is not accompanied by delusions, and frequently no change will have been noticed in the individual prior to the commission of the act, and consequently, says Dr Luff, "there is much difference of opinion as to the responsibility of the individual" (ii. 297). Among the acts spoken of Dr Luff mentions a propensity to set fire to furniture, houses, etc. All this, though written in 1895, might serve as a commentary on the Suffragette agitation of recent years. The renowned French professor, Dr Paul Janet ("Les Hysteriques," 1894) thus defined hysteria: "Hysteria is a mental affection belonging to the large group of diseases due to cerebral weakness and debility. Its physical symptoms are somewhat indefinite, consisting chiefly in a general diminution of nutrition. It is largely characterised by moral symptoms, chief of which is an impairment of the faculty of psychological synthesis, an abolition and a contraction of the field of consciousness. This manifests itself in a peculiar manner and by a certain number of elementary phenomena. Thus sensations and images are no longer perceived, and appear to be blotted out from the individual perception, a tendency which results in their persistent and complete separation from the personality in some cases and in the formation of many independent groups. This series of psychological facts alternate the one with the other or co-exist. Finally this synthetic defect favours the formation of certain independent ideas, which develop complete in themselves, and unattached from the control of the consciousness of the personality. These ideas show themselves in affections possessing very various and unique characteristics." According to Mr A. S. Millar, F.R.C.S.E. (*Encyclopædia Medica*, vol. v.), "Hysteria is that . . . condition in which there is imagination, imitation, or exaggeration. . . . It occurs mostly in females and persons of nervous temperament, and is due to some nervous derangement, which may or may not be pathological." Sir James Paget ("Clinical Lectures on Mimicry") says also that hysterical patients are mostly females of nervous temperament. "They think of themselves constantly, are fond of telling everyone of their troubles and thus court sympathy, for which they have a morbid craving. Will power is deficient in one direction, though some have it very strongly where their interests are concerned." He thinks the term "hysteria" in the sense now employed incorrect, and would substitute "mimicry." "The will should be controlled by the intellect," observes Dr G. F. Still of King's College Hospital, "rather than by the emotions and the lack of this control appears to be at the root of some, at least, of the manifestations of hysteria."

Dr Thomas Buzzard, above mentioned, thus summarises the mental symptoms: "The intelligence may be apparently of good quality, the patient evincing sometimes remarkable quickness of apprehension; but carefully tested it is found to be wanting in the essentials of the highest class of mental power. The memory may be good, but the judgment is weak and the ability to concentrate the attention for any length of time upon a subject is absent. So also regard for accuracy, and the energy necessary to ensure it in any work that is undertaken, is deficient. The emotions are excited with undue readiness and when aroused are incapable of control. Tears are occasioned not only by pathetic ideas but by ridiculous subjects and peals of laughter may incongruously greet some tragic announcement, or the converse may take place. The ordinary signs of emotion may be absent and replaced by an attack of syncope, convulsion, pain or paralysis. Perhaps more constant than any other phenomenon in hysteria is a pronounced desire for the sympathy and interest of others. This is evidently only one of the most characteristic qualities of femininity, uncontrolled by the action of the higher nervous centres which in a healthy state keep it in subjection. There is very frequently not only a deficient regard for truthfulness, but a proneness to active deception and dishonesty. So common is this, that the various phases of hysteria are often assumed to be simple examples of voluntary simulation and the title of disease refused to the condition. But it seems more reasonable to refer the symptoms to impairment of the highly complex nervous processes which form the physiological side of the moral faculties" (Quain's *Dictionary of Medicine*, 1902).

"It is not uncommon to find hysteria in females accompanied by an utter indifference and insensibility to sexual relations. Premature cessation of ovulation is a frequent determining cause. In cases where the ovaries are absent the change from girl to woman, which normally takes place at puberty, does not occur. The girl grows but does not develop, a masculine appearance supervenes, the voice becomes manly and harsh, sexual passion is absent, the health remains good. The most violent instances of hysteria are in young women of the most robust and masculine constitution" (John Mason Good, M.D., "Study of Medicine," 1822). Other determining causes are given, as painful impressions, long fasting, strong emotions, imitation, luxury, ill-directed education and unhappy surroundings, celibacy, where not of choice but enforced by circumstances, unfortunate marriages, long-continued trouble, fright, worry, overwork, disappointment and such like nervous perturbations, all which causes predispose to hysteria. "It attacks childless women more frequently than mothers and particularly young widows," and, says Dr J. Mason Good, "more especially still those who are constitutionally inclined to that morbid salacity which has often been called nymphomania . . . the surest remedy is a happy marriage" ("Study of Medicine," 1822, iii. 531). Hysteria is, in common with other nervous disorders, essentially a hereditary malady, and Briquet ("Traité de l'hysterie," 1899) gives statistics to show that in nine cases out of ten hysterical parents have hysterical children. Dr Paul Sainton of the Faculty of Medicine, Paris, says: "The appearance of a symptom of hysteria generally proves that the malady has already existed for some time though latent. The name of a provocative agent of hysteria is given to any circumstance which suddenly reveals the malady but the real cause of the disorder is a hereditary disposition. If the real cause is unique, the provocative agents are numberless. The moral emotions, grief, fright, anger and other psychic disturbances are the most frequent causes of hysterical affections and in every walk of life subjects are equally liable to attacks."

Hysteria may appear at any age. It is common with children, especially during the five or six years preceding puberty. Of thirty-three cases under twelve years which came under Dr Still's notice, twenty-three were in children over eight years. Hysteria in women is most frequent between the ages of fifteen and thirty, and most frequently of all between fifteen and twenty. As a rule there is a tendency to cessation after the "change." It frequently happens, however, that the disease is continued into an advanced period of life.

"There is a constant change," says Professor Albert Moll ("Das nervöse Weib," p. 165), "from a cheerful to a depressed mood. From being free and merry the woman in a short time becomes sulky and sad. While a moment before she was capable of entertaining a whole company without pause, talking to each member about that which interested him, shortly afterwards she does not speak a word more. I may mention the well-worn example of the refusal of a new hat as being capable of converting the most lively mood into its opposite. The weakness of will shows itself here in that the nervous woman [by "nervous" Dr Moll means what is commonly termed "hysterical"] cannot, like the normal one, command the expression of her emotions. She can laugh uninterruptedly over the most indifferent matter until she falls into veritable laughing fits. The crying fits which we sometimes observe belong to the same category. When the nervous woman is excited about anything she exhibits outbreaks of fury wanting all the characteristics of womanhood, and she is not able to prevent these emotional outbursts. In the same way just as the emotions weaken the will and the woman cannot suppress this or that action, it is noticeable in many nervous women that quite independently of these emotions there is a tendency to continuous alterations in their way of acting. It has been noticed as characteristic of many nervous persons that their only consistency lies in their inconsistency. But this must in no way be applied to all nervous persons. On this disposition, discoverable in the nature of so many nervous women, rests the craving for change as manifested in the continual search for new pleasures, theatres, concerts, parties, tours, and other things (p. 147). Things that to the normal woman are indifferent or to which she has, in a sense, accustomed herself, are to the nervous woman a source of constant worry. Although she may perfectly well know that the circumstances of herself and her husband are the most brilliant and that it is unnecessary for her to trouble herself in the least about her material position as regards the future, nevertheless the idea of financial ruin constantly troubles her. Thus if she is a millionaire's wife she never escapes from constant worry. Similarly the nervous woman creates troubles out of things that are unavoidable. If in the course of years she gets more wrinkles, and her attraction for man diminishes, this may easily become a source of lasting sorrow for the nervous woman."

We now have to consider a point which is being continually urged by Feminists in the present day when confronted with the pathological mental symptoms so commonly observed in women which are usually regarded as having their origin in hysteria. We often hear it said by Feminists in answer to arguments based on the above fact: "Oh, but men can also suffer from hysteria!" "In England," says Dr Buzzard, "hysteria is comparatively rarely met with in males, the female sex being much more prone to the affection." The proportion of males to females in hysteria is, according to Dr Pitrè ("Clinical Essay on Hysteria," 1891), 1 to 3; according to Bodensheim, 1 to 10; and according to Briquet, 1 to 20. The author of the article on Hysteria in *The Encyclopædia Britannica* (11th edition, 1911) also gives 1 to 20 as the numerical proportion between male and female cases. Dr Pitrè, in the work above cited, gives 82 per cent. of cases of convulsions in women as against 22 in men. But in all this, under the concept hysteria are included, and indeed chiefly referred to, various physical symptoms of a convulsive and epileptic character which are quite distinct from the mental conditions rightly or wrongly connected, or even identified, with hysteria in the popular mind, and by many medical authorities. But even as regards hysteria in the former sense of the word, a sharp line of distinction based on a diagnosis of cases was long ago drawn by medical men between *hysteria masculina* and *hysteria fœminina*, and in the present day eminent authorities —*e.g.* Dr Bernard Holländer—would deny that the symptoms occasionally diagnosed as hysteria in men are identical with or due to the same causes as the somewhat similar conditions known in women under the name.

After all, this whole question in its broader bearings is more a question of common-sense observation than one for medical experts.

What we are here chiefly concerned with as "hysteria" (in accordance with popular usage of the term) are certain pathological mental symptoms in women open to everybody's observation, and denied by no one unprejudiced by Feminist views. Every impartial person has only to cast his eye round his female acquaintance, and to recall the various women, of all classes, conditions and nationalities, that he may have come in contact with in the course of his life, to recognise those symptoms of mental instability commonly called hysterical, as obtaining in at least a proportion of one to every four or five women he has known, in a marked and unmistakable degree. The proportion given is, in fact, stated in an official report to the Prussian Government issued some ten years back as that noticeable among female clerks, post office servants and other women employed in the Prussian Civil Service. Certainly as regards women in general, the observation of the present writer, and others whom he has questioned on the subject, would seem to indicate that the proportions given in the Prussian Civil Service report as regards the number of women afflicted in this way are rather under than over stated.[44:1] There are many medical men who aver that no woman is entirely free from such symptoms at least immediately before and during the menstrual period. The head surgeon at a well-known London hospital informed a friend of mine that he could always tell when this period was on or approaching with his nurses, by the mental change which came over them.

[44:1] The insanities mentioned above are the extremes. There are mental disturbances of less severity constantly occurring which are connected with the regular menstrual period as well as with disordered menstruation, with pregnancy, with parturition, with lactation, and especially with the change of life.

Now these pathological symptoms noticeable in a slight and more or less unimportant degree in the vast majority, if not indeed in all women, and in a marked pathological degree in a large proportion of women, it is scarcely too much to say do not occur at all in men. I have indeed known, I think, two men, and only two, in the course of my life, exhibiting mental symptoms analogous to those commonly called "hysterical" in women. On the other hand my own experience, and it is not alone, is that very few women with whom I have come into more or less frequent contact, socially or otherwise, have not at times shown the symptoms referred to in a marked degree. If, therefore, we are to admit the bare possibility of men being afflicted in a similar way it must be conceded that such cases represent such *raræ aves* as to be negligible for practical purposes.

A curious thing in pronounced examples of this mental instability in women is that the symptoms are often so very similar in women of quite different birth, surroundings and nationality. I can recall at the present moment three cases, each different as regards birth, class, and in one case nationality, and yet who are liable to develop the same symptoms under the influence of quite similar *idées fixes*.

But it seems hardly necessary to labour the point in question at greater length. The whole experience of mankind since the dawn of written records confirmed by, as above said, that of every living person not specially committed to the theories of Modern Feminism, bears witness alike to the prevalence of what we may term the hysterical mind in woman and to her general mental frailty. It is not for nothing that women and children have always been classed together. This view, based as it is on the unanimous experience of mankind and confirmed by the observation of all independent persons, has, I repeat, not been challenged before the appearance of the present Feminist Movement and hardly by anyone outside the ranks of that movement.

It is not proposed here to dilate at length on the fact, often before insisted upon, of the absence throughout history of the signs of genius, and, with a few exceptions, of conspicuous talent, in the human female, in art, science, literature, invention or "affairs." The fact is incontestable, and if it be argued that this absence in women, of genius or even of a high degree of talent, is no proof of the inferiority of the average woman to the average man the answer is obvious.

Apart from conclusive proof, the fact of the existence in all periods of civilisation, and even under the higher barbarism, of exceptionally gifted men, and never of a correspondingly gifted woman, does undoubtedly afford an indication of inferiority of the average woman as regards the average man. From the height of the mountain peaks we may, other things equal, undoubtedly conclude the existence of a tableland beneath them in the same tract of country whence they arise. I have already, in the present chapter, besides elsewhere, referred to the fallacy that intellectual or other fundamental inferiority in woman existing at the present day is traceable to any alleged repression in the past, since (Weissmann and his denial of transmission of acquired characteristics apart), assuming for the sake of the argument such repression to have really attained the extent alleged, and its effects to have been transmitted to future generations, it is against all the laws of heredity that such transmission should have taken place *through the female line alone,* as is contended by the advocates of this theory. Referring to this point, Herbert Spencer has expressed the conviction of most scientific thinkers on the subject when he declares a difference between the mental powers of men and women to result from "a physiological necessity, and [that] no amount of culture can obliterate it." He further observes (the passages occur in a letter of his to John Stuart Mill) that "the relative deficiency of the female mind is in just those most complex faculties, intellectual and moral, which have political action for their sphere."

One of the points as regards the inferiority of women which Feminists are willing and even eager to concede, and it is the only point of which this can be said, is that of physical weakness. The reason why they should be particularly anxious to emphasise this deficiency in the sex is not difficult to discern. It is the only possible semblance of an argument which can be plausibly brought forward to justify female privileges in certain directions. It does not really do so, but it is the sole pretext which they can adduce with any show of reason at all. Now it may be observed (1) that the general frailty of woman would militate *coetaris paribus,* against their own dogma of the intellectual equality between the sexes; (2) that this physical weakness is more particularly a muscular weakness, since constitutionally the organism of the human female has enormous power of resistance and resilience, in general, far greater than that of man (see below, pp. 125-128). It is a matter of common observation that the average woman can pass through strains and recover in a way few men can do. But as we shall have occasion to revert to these two points at greater length later on, we refrain from saying more here.

How then, after consideration, shall we judge of the Feminist thesis, affirmed and reaffirmed, insisted upon by so many as an incontrovertible axiom, that woman is the equal, intellectually and morally, if not physically, of man? Surely that it has all the characteristics of a true dogma. Its votaries might well say with Tertullian, *credo quia absurdum.* It contradicts the whole experience of mankind in the past. It is refuted by all impartial observation in the present. The facts which undermine it are seriously denied by none save those committed to the dogma in question. Like all dogmas, it is supported by "bluff." In this case the "bluff" is to the effect that it is the "part, mark, business, lot" (as the Latin grammars of our youth would have had it) of the "advanced" man who considers himself up to date, and not "Early Victorian," to regard it as unchallengeable. Theological dogmas are backed up by the bluff of authority, either of scriptures or of churches. This dogma of the Feminist cult is not vouchsafed by the authority of a Communion of saints but by that of the Communion of advanced persons up to date. Unfortunately dogma does not sit so well upon the community of advanced persons up to date—who otherwise profess to, and generally do, bring the tenets they hold to the bar of reason and critical test—as it does on a church or community of saints who suppose themselves to be individually or collectively in communication with wisdom from on high. Be this as it may, the "advanced man" who would claim to be "up to date" has to swallow this dogma and digest it as best he can. He may secretly, it is true, spew it out of his mouth, but in public, at least, he must make a pretence of accepting it without flinching.

CHAPTER III
THE ANTI-MAN CRUSADE

We have already pointed out that Modern Feminism has two sides or aspects. The first formulates definite political, juridical and economic demands on the grounds of justice, equity, equality and so forth, as general principles; the second does not formulate in so many words definite demands as general principles, but seems to exploit the traditional notions of chivalry based on male sex sentiment, in favour of according women special privileges on the ground of their sex, in the law, and still more in the administration of the law. For the sake of brevity we call the first *Political Feminism*, for, although its demands are not confined to the political sphere, it is first and foremost a political movement, and its typical claim at the present time, the Franchise, is a purely political one; and the second *Sentimental Feminism*, inasmuch as it commonly does not profess to be based on any general principle whatever, whether of equity or otherwise, but relies exclusively on the traditional and conventional sex sentiment of Man towards Woman. It may be here premised that most Political Feminists, however much they may refuse to admit it, are at heart also Sentimental Feminists. Sentimental Feminists, on the other hand, are not invariably Political Feminists, although the majority of them undoubtedly are so to a greater or lesser extent. Logically, as we shall have occasion to insist upon later on, the principles professedly at the root of Political Feminism are in flagrant contradiction with any that can justify Sentimental Feminism.

Now both the orders of Feminism referred to have been active for more than a generation past in fomenting a crusade against the male sex—an Anti-Man Crusade. Their efforts have been largely successful owing to a fact to which attention has, perhaps, not enough been called. In the case of other classes, or bodies of persons, having community of interests this common interest invariably interprets itself in a sense of class, caste, or race solidarity. The class or caste has a certain *esprit de corps* in its own interest. The whole of history largely turns on the conflict of economic classes based on a common feeling obtaining between members of the respective classes;

on a small scale, we see the same thing in the solidarity of a particular trade or profession. But it is unnecessary to do more than call attention here to this fundamental sociological law upon which alike the class struggles of history, and of modern times, the patriotism of states from the city-state of the ancient world to the national state of the modern world, is based. Now note the peculiar manner in which this law manifests itself in the sex question of the present day. While Modern Feminism has succeeded in establishing a powerful sex-solidarity amongst a large section of women as against men, there is not only no sex-solidarity of men as against women, but, on the contrary, the prevalence of an altogether opposed sentiment. Men hate their brother-men in their capacity of male persons. In any conflict of interests between a man and a woman, male public opinion, often in defiance of the most obvious considerations of equity, sides with the woman, and glories in doing so. Here we seem to have a very flagrant contradiction with, as has already been said, one of the most fundamental sociological laws. The explanations of the phenomena in question are, of course, ready to hand:—Tradition of chivalry, feelings, perhaps inherited, dating possibly back to the prehuman stage of man's evolution, derived from the competition of the male with his fellow-male for the possession of the coveted female, etc.

These explanations may have a measure of validity, but I must confess they are to me scarcely adequate to account for the intense hatred which the large section of men seem to entertain towards their fellow-males in the world of to-day, and their eagerness to champion the female in the sex war which the Woman's "sex union," as it has been termed, has declared of recent years. Whatever may be the explanation, and I confess I cannot find one completely satisfactory, the fact remains. A Woman's Movement unassisted by man, still more if opposed energetically by the public opinion of a solid phalanx of the manhood of any country, could not possibly make any headway. As it is, we see the legislature, judges, juries, parsons, specially those of the nonconformist persuasion, all vie with one another in denouncing the villainy and baseness of the male person, and ever devising ways and means to make his life hard for him. To these are joined a host of literary men and journalists of varying degrees of reputation who contribute their quota to the stream of anti-manism in the shape of novels, storiettes, essays, and articles, the design of which is to paint man as a base, contemptible creature, as at once a knave and an imbecile, a bird of prey and a sheep in wolf's clothing, and all as a foil to the glorious majesty of Womanhood. There are not wanting artists who are pressed into this service. The picture of the Thames Embankment at night, of the drowned unfortunate with the angel's face, the lady and gentleman in evening dress who have just got out of their cab—the lady with uplifted hands bending over the dripping form, and the callous and brutal gentleman turning aside to light a cigarette—this is a typical specimen of Feminist didactic art. By these means, which have been carried on with increasing ardour for a couple of generations past, what we may term the anti-man cultus has been made to flourish and to bear fruit till we find nowadays all recent legislation affecting the relations between the sexes carrying its impress, and the whole of the judiciary and magistracy acting as its priests and ministrants.

On the subject of Anti-man legislation, I have already written at length elsewhere,[55:1] but for the sake of completeness I state the case briefly here. (1) The marriage laws of England to-day are a monument of Feminist sex partiality. If I may be excused the paradox, the partiality of the marriage laws begins with the law relating to breach of promise, which, as is well known, enables a woman to punish a man vindictively for refusing to marry her after having once engaged himself to her. I ought to add, and this, oftentimes, however good his grounds may be for doing so. Should the woman commit perjury, in these cases, she is never prosecuted for the offence. Although the law of breach of promise exists also for the man, it is well known to be totally ineffective and practically a dead letter. It should be remarked that, however gross the misrepresentations or undue influences on the part of the woman may have been to induce the man to marry her, they do not cause her to lose her right to compensation. As, for instance, where an experienced woman of the world of thirty or forty entraps a boy scarcely out of his teens. (2) Again, according to the law of England, the right to maintenance accrues solely to the woman. Formerly this privilege was made dependent on her cohabitation with the man and generally decent behaviour to him. Now even these limitations cease to be operative, while the man is liable to imprisonment and confiscation of any property he may have. A wife is now at full liberty to leave her husband, while she retains her right to get her husband sent to gaol if he refuses to maintain her—to put the matter shortly, the law imposes upon the wife no legally enforceable duties whatever *towards* her husband. The one thing which it will enforce with iron vigour is the wife's right of maintenance *against* her husband. In the case of a man of the well-to-do classes, the man's property is confiscated by the law in favour of his wife. In the case of a working man the law compels her husband to do *corvée* for her, as the feudal serf had to do for his lord. The wife, on the other hand, however wealthy, is not compelled to give a farthing towards the support of her husband, even though disabled by sickness or by accident; the single exception in the latter case being should he become chargeable to the parish, in which case the wife would have to pay the authorities a pauper's rate for his maintenance. In a word, a wife has complete possession and control over any property she may possess, as well as over her earnings; the husband, on the other hand, is liable to confiscation of capitalised property or earnings at the behest of the law courts in favour of his wife. A wife may even make her husband bankrupt on the ground of money she alleges that she lent him; a husband, on the other hand, has no claim against his wife for any money advanced, since a husband is supposed to *give*, and not to *lend*, his wife money, or other valuables. (3) The law affords the wife a right to commit torts against third parties—*e.g.* libels and slanders—the husband alone being responsible, and this rule applies even although the wife is living apart from her husband, who is wholly without knowledge of her misdeeds. With the exception of murder, a wife is held by the law to be guiltless of practically any crime committed in the presence of her husband. (4) No man can obtain a legal separation or divorce from his wife (save under the Licensing Act of 1902, a Police Court separation for habitual drunkenness alone) without a costly process in the High Court. Every wife can obtain, if not a divorce, at least a legal separation, by going whining to the nearest police court, for a few shillings, which her husband, of course, has to pay. The latter, it is needless to say, is mulcted in alimony at the "discretion of the Court." This "discretion" is very often of a queer character for the luckless husband. Thus, a working man earning only twenty shillings a week may easily find himself in the position of having to pay from seven to ten shillings a week to a shrew out of his wages.

[55:1] Cf. *Fortnightly Review*, November 1911, "A Creature of Privilege," also a pamphlet (collaboration) entitled "The Legal Subjection of Men." Twentieth Century Press, reprinted by New Age Press, 1908.

In cases where a wife proceeds to file a petition for divorce, the way is once more smoothed for her by the law, at the husband's expense. He has to advance her money to enable her to fight him. Should the case come on for hearing the husband finds the scale still more weighted against him; every slander of his wife is assumed to be true until he has proved its falsity, the slightest act or a word during a moment of irritation, even a long time back, being twisted into what is termed "legal cruelty," even though such has been provoked by a long course of ill treatment and neglect on the part of the wife. The husband and his witnesses can be indicted for perjury for the slightest exaggeration or inaccuracy in their statements, while the most calculated falsity in the evidence of the wife and her witnesses is passed over. Not the grossest allegation on the part of the wife against the husband, even though proved in court to be false, is sufficient ground for the husband to refuse to take her back again, or from preventing the court from confiscating his property if he resists doing so. Knowledge of the unfairness of the court to the husband, as all lawyers are aware, prevents a large number of men from defending divorce actions brought by their wives. A point should here be mentioned as regards the action of a husband for damages against the seducer of his wife. Such damages obviously belong to the husband as compensation for his destroyed home life. Now these damages our modern judges in their feminist zeal have converted into a fund for endowing the adulteress, depriving the husband of any compensation whatever for the wrong done him. He may not touch the income derived from the money awarded him by the jury, which is handed over by the court to his divorced wife. It would take us too long to go through all the privileges, direct and indirect, conferred by statute or created by the rulings of judges and the practice of the courts, in favour of the wife against the husband. It is the more unnecessary to go into them here as they may be found in detail with illustrative cases in the aforesaid pamphlet in which I collaborated, entitled "The Legal Subjection of Men" (mentioned in the footnote to p. 55).

At this point it may be well to say a word on the one rule of the divorce law which Feminists are perennially trotting out as a proof of the shocking injustice of the marriage law to women: that to obtain her divorce the woman has to prove cruelty in addition to adultery against her husband, while in the case of the husband it is sufficient to prove adultery alone. Now to make of this rule a grievance for the woman is, I submit, evidence of the destitution of the Feminist case. In default of any real injustice pressing on the woman the Feminist is constrained to make as much capital as possible out of the merest semblance of a grievance he can lay his hand on. The reasons for this distinction which the law draws between the husband and the wife, it is obvious enough, are perfectly well grounded. It is based mainly on the simple fact that while a woman by her adultery may foist upon her husband a bastard which he will be compelled by law to support as his own child, in the husband's case of having an illegitimate child the wife and her property are not affected. Now in a society such as ours is, based upon private property-holding, it is only natural, I submit, that the law should take account of this fact. But not only is this rule of law almost certainly doomed to repeal in the near future, but in even the present day, while it still nominally exists, it is practically a dead letter in the divorce court, since any trivial act of which the wife chooses to complain is strained by the court into evidence of cruelty in the legal and technical sense. As the matter stands, the practical effect of the rule is a much greater injustice to the husband than to the wife, since the former often finds himself convicted of "cruelty" which is virtually nothing at all, in order that the wife's petition may be granted, and which is often made the excuse by Feminist judges for depriving the husband of the custody of his children. Misconduct on the wife's part, or neglect of husband and children, does not weigh with the court which will not on that ground grant relief to the husband from his obligation for maintenance, etc. On the other hand, neglect of the wife by the husband is made a ground for judicial separation with the usual consequences—alimony, etc. "Thus," as it has been put, "between the upper and the nether millstone, cruelty on the one hand, neglect on the other, the unhappy husband can be legally ground to pieces, whether he does anything or whether he does nothing." Personal violence on the part of the husband is severely punished; on the part of a wife she will be let off with impunity. Even if she should in an extreme case be imprisoned, the husband, if a poor man, on her release will be compelled to take her back to live with him. The case came under the notice of the writer a few years ago in which a humane magistrate was constrained to let off a woman who had nearly murdered a husband on the condition of her graciously consenting to a separation, but she had presumably still to be supported by her victim.

The decision in the notorious Jackson case precluded the husband from compelling his wife to obey an order of the court for the restitution of conjugal rights. The persistent Feminist tendency of all case-law is illustrated by a decision of the House of Lords in 1894 in reference to the law of Scotland constituting desertion for four years a ground *ipso facto* for a divorce with the right of remarriage. Here divorce was refused to a man whose wife had left him for four years and taken her child with her. The Law Lords justified their own interpretation of the law on the ground that the man did not really want her to come back. But inasmuch as this plea can be started in every case where it cannot be proved that the husband had absolutely grovelled before his wife, imploring her to return, and possibly even then—since the sincerity even of this grovelling might conceivably be called in question—it is clear that the decision practically rendered this old Scottish law inoperative for the husband.

As regards the offence of bigamy, for which a man commonly receives a heavy sentence of penal servitude, I think I may venture to state, without risking contradiction, that no woman during recent years has been imprisoned for this offence. The statute law, while conferring distinct privileges upon married women as to the control of their property, and for trading separately and apart from their husbands, renders them exempt from the ordinary liabilities incurred by a male trader as regards proceedings under the Debtors Acts and the Bankruptcy Law. See Acts of 1822 (45 & 46 Vict. c. 75); 1893 (56 & 57 Vict. c. 63), and cases Scott *v.* Morley, 57 L.J.R.Q.B. 43. L.R. 20 Q.B.D. In *re* Hannah Lines *exparte* Lester C.A. (1893), 2. 2. B. 113.

In the case of Lady Bateman *v.* Faber and others reported in Chancery Appeal Cases (1898 Law Reports) the Master of the Rolls (Sir N. Lindley) is reported to have said: "The authorities showed that a married woman could not by hook or by crook—even by her own fraud—deprive herself of restraint upon anticipation. He would say nothing as to the policy of the law, but it had been affirmed by the Married Woman's Property Act" (the Act of 1882 above referred to) "and the result was that a married woman could play fast and loose to an extent to which no other person could." (*N.B.*—Presumably a male person.)

It has indeed been held, to such a length does the law extend its protection and privileges to the female, that even the concealment by a wife from the husband at the time of marriage that she was then pregnant by another man was no ground for declaring the marriage null and void.

The above may be taken as a fair all-round, although by no means an exhaustive, statement of the present one-sided condition of the civil law as regards the relation of husband and wife. We will now pass on to the consideration of the relative incidence of the criminal law on the two sexes. We will begin with the crime of murder. The law of murder is still ostensibly the same for both sexes, but in effect the application of its provisions in the two cases is markedly different. As, however, these differences lie, as just stated, not in the law itself but rather in its administration, we can only give in this place, where we are dealing with the principles of law rather than with their application, a general formula of the mode in which the administration of the law of murder proceeds, which, briefly stated, is as follows: The evidence even to secure conviction in the case of a woman must be many times stronger than that which would suffice to hang a man. Should a conviction be obtained, the death penalty, though pronounced, is not given effect to, the female prisoner being almost invariably reprieved. In most cases where there is conviction at all, it is for manslaughter and not for murder, when a light or almost nominal sentence is passed. Cases confirming what is here said will be given later on. There is one point, however, to be observed here, and that is the crushing incidence of the law of libel. This means that no case of any woman, however notoriously guilty on the evidence, can be quoted, after she has been acquitted by a Feminist jury, as the law holds such to be innocent and provides them with "a remedy" in a libel action. Now, seeing that most women accused of murder are acquitted irrespective of the evidence, it is clear that the writer is fatally handicapped so far as confirmation of his thesis by cases is concerned.

Women are to all intents and purposes allowed to harass men, when they conceive they have a grievance, at their own sweet will, the magistrate usually telling their victim that he cannot interfere. In the opposite case, that of a man harassing a woman, the latter has invariably to find sureties for his future good behaviour, or else go to gaol.

One of the most infamous enactments indicative of Feminist sex bias is the Criminal Law Amendment Act of 1886. The Act itself was led up to with the usual effect by an unscrupulous newspaper agitation in the Feminist and Puritan interest, designed to create a panic in the public mind, under the influence of which legislation of this description can generally be rushed through Parliament. The reckless disregard of the commonest principles of justice and common-sense of this abominable statute may be seen in the shameless sex privilege it accords the female in the matter of seduction. Under its provisions a boy of fourteen years can be prosecuted and sent to gaol for an offence to which he has been instigated by a girl just under sixteen years, whom the law, of course, on the basis of the aforesaid sex privilege, holds guiltless. The outrageous infamy of this provision is especially apparent when we consider the greater precocity of the average girl as compared with the average boy of this age.

We come now to the latest piece of Anti-man legislation, the so-called *White Slave Trade Act of 1912* (Criminal Law Amendment Act 1912, 2 & 3 Geo. V. c. 20). This statute was, as usual, rushed through the legislature on the wave of factitious public excitement organised for the purpose, and backed up by the usual faked statements and exaggerated allegations, the whole matter being three parts bogus and deliberate lying. The alleged dangers of the unprotected female were, for the object of the agitation, purposely exaggerated in the proverbial proportion of the mountain to the molehill. But as regards many of those most eager in promoting this piece of Anti-man legislation, there were probably special psychological reasons to account for their attitude. The special features of the Bill, the Act in question, are (1) increased powers given to the police in the matter of arrest on suspicion, and (2) the flogging clauses.

Up till now the flogging of garrotters was justified against opponents, by its upholders, on the ground of the peculiarly brutal nature of the offence of highway robbery with violence. It should be noted that in the Act in question no such excuse can apply, for it is appointed to be inflicted for offences which, whatever else they may be, do not in their nature involve violence, and hence which cannot be described as brutal in the ordinary sense of the term. The Anti-man nature of the whole measure, as of the agitation itself which preceded it, is conclusively evidenced by the fact that while it is well known that the number of women gaining a living by "procuration" is much greater than the number of men engaged therein, comparatively little vituperation was heard against the female delinquents in the matter, and certainly none of the vitriolic ferocity that was poured out upon the men alleged to participate in the traffic. A corresponding distinction was represented in the measure itself by the allocation of the torture of the lash to men alone. It is clear, therefore, that the zeal for the suppression of the traffic in question was not the sole motive in the ardour of the flogging fraternity. Even the Anti-manism at the back of the whole of this class of legislation seems insufficient to account for the outbreak of bestial blood-lust, for the tigerish ferocity, of which the flogging clauses in the Act are the outcome. There is, I take it, no doubt that psychical sexual aberration plays a not inconsiderable part in many of those persons—in a word, that they are labouring under some degree of homo-sexual Sadism. The lustful glee on the part of the aforesaid persons which greets the notion of the partial flaying alive, for that is what the "cat" means, of some poor wretch who has succumbed to the temptation of getting his livelihood by an improper method, is hardly to be explained on any other hypothesis. Experts allege that traces of psycho-sexual aberration are latent in many persons where it would be least expected, and it is, *prima facie*, likely enough that these latent tendencies in both men and women should become active under the cover of an agitation in favour of purity and anti-sexuality, to the point of gratifying itself with the thought of torture inflicted upon men. A psycho-sexual element of another kind doubtless also plays a not unimportant rôle in the agitation of "ladies" in favour of that abomination, "social purity," which, being interpreted, generally means lubricity turned upside down. The fiery zeal manifested by many of those ladies for the suppression of the male sex is assuredly not without its pathological significance.

The monstrosity of the recent *White Slave Traffic* enactment and its savage anti-male vindictiveness is shown not merely, as already observed, in the agitation which preceded it, with its exaggerated vilification of the male offenders in the matter of procuration and its passing over with comparative slight censure the more numerous female offenders, or in the general spirit animating the Act itself, but it is noticeable in the very preposterous exaggeration of its provisions. For example, in the section dealing with the *souteneur*, the framers of this Act, and the previous

Criminal Law Amendment Acts to which this latest one is merely supplementary, are not satisfied with penalising the man who has no other means of subsistence beyond what he derives from the wages of some female friend's prostitution, but they strike with impartial rigour the man who knowingly lives *wholly or in part* from such a source. If, therefore, the clause were taken in its strict sense, any poor out-at-elbow man who accepted the hospitality of a woman of doubtful virtue in the matter of a drink, or a dinner, would put himself within the pale of this clause in the Act, and might be duly flayed by the "cat" in consequence. The most flagrant case occurred in a London police court in March 1913, in which a youth of eighteen years, against whose general character nothing was alleged and who was known to be in employment as a carman, was sentenced to a month's hard labour under the following circumstances:—It was reported that he had been living with a woman apparently considerably older than himself, whom admittedly he had supported by his own exertions and, when this was insufficient, even by the pawning of his clothes, and whom as soon as he discovered she was earning money by prostitution he had left. Would it be believed that a prosecution was instituted by the police against this young man under the iniquitous White Slave Traffic Act? But what seems still more incredible is that the magistrate, presumably a sane gentleman, after admitting that the poor fellow was "more sinned against than sinning," did not hesitate to pass on him a sentence of one month's hard labour!!! Of course the woman, who was the head and front of the offending, if offending there was, remained untouched. The above is a mild specimen of "justice" as meted out in our police courts, "for men only"! Quite recently there was a case in the north of England of a carter, who admittedly worked at his calling but who, it was alleged, was assisted by women with whom he had lived. Now this unfortunate man was sentenced to a long term of imprisonment plus flogging. For the judges, of course, any extension of their power over the prisoner in the dock is a godsend. It is quite evident that they are revelling in their new privilege to inflict torture. One of them had the shamelessness recently to boast of the satisfaction it gave him and to sneer at those of his colleagues who did not make full use of their judicial powers in this direction.

The bogus nature of the reasons urged in favour of the most atrocious clauses of this abominable Act came out clearly enough in the speeches of the official spokesmen of the Government in its favour. For example, Lord Haldane in the House of Lords besought the assembled peers to bethink themselves of the unhappy victim of the *souteneur*. He drew a picture of how a heartless bully might beat, starve and otherwise ill treat his victim, besides taking away her earnings. He omitted to explain how the heartless bully in a free country could coerce his "victim" to remain with him against her will. He ignored the existence of the police, or of a whole army of social purity busybodies, and vigilance societies for whom her case would be a tasty morsel only too eagerly snapped at. If the "victim" does not avail herself of any of those means of escape, so ready to her hand, the presumption is that she prefers the company of her alleged brutal tyrant to that of the chaste Puritan ladies of the vigilance societies. To those who follow the present state of artificially fomented public opinion in the matter, Lord Haldane's suggestion that there was any danger of the precious "victim" not being sufficiently slobbered over, will seem to be not without a touch of humour. Furthermore, as illustrating the utter illogicality of the line taken by the promoters of the Act, for whom Lord Haldane acted as the mouthpiece, we have only to note the fact that the measure does not limit the penalties awarded to cases accompanied by circumstances of aggravation such as Lord Haldane pictures, which it might easily have done, but extends it impartially to all cases whether accompanied by cruelty or not. We can hardly imagine that a man of Lord Haldane's intellectual power and general humanity should not have been aware of the hollowness of the case he had to put as an official advocate, and of the rottenness of the conventional arguments he had to state in its support. When confronted with the unquestionably true contention that corporal punishments, especially such as are of a savage and vindictive kind, are degrading alike to the inflicters of them and to those who are their victims, he replied that criminals in the cases in question were already so degraded that they could not be degraded further. One would imagine he could hardly have failed to know that he was talking pernicious twaddle. It is obvious that this argument, in addition to its being untrue, in fact opens the floodgates to brutal penal legislation all round, so far at least as the more serious offences are concerned. One could equally well assert of murder, burglary, even *abus de confidence* in some cases, and other offences, that the perpetrators of them must be so degraded that no amount of brutal punishment could degrade them further. Everybody can regard the crime to which he has a pet aversion more than other crimes as indicating the perpetrator thereof to be outside the pale of humanity.

But as regards the particular case in point, let us for a moment clear our minds of cant upon the subject. Procuration and also living on the proceeds of prostitution may be morally abominable methods of securing a livelihood, though even here, as in most other offences, there may be circumstances of palliation in individual cases. But after all is said and done, it is doubtful whether, apart from any fraud or misrepresentation, which, of course, places it altogether in a different category, these ought to be regarded as *criminal* offences. To offer facilities or to act as an agent for women who are anxious to lead a "gay life," or even to suggest such a course to women, *so long as prostitution itself is not recognised by the law as crime*, however reprehensible morally, would scarcely seem to transcend the limits of legitimate individual liberty. In any case, the constituting of such an action a crime must surely open out an altogether new principle in jurisprudence, and one of far-reaching consequences. The same remarks apply even more forcibly to the question of sharing the earnings of a prostitute. Prostitution *per se* is not in the eyes of the law a crime or even a misdemeanour. The woman who makes her living as a prostitute is under the protection of the law, and the money she receives from her customer is recognised as her property. If she, however, in the exercise of her right of free disposition of that property, gives some of it to a male friend, that friend, by the mere acceptance of a free gift, becomes a criminal in the eyes of the law. Anything more preposterous, judging by all hitherto recognised principles of jurisprudence, can scarcely be imagined. Even from the moral point of view of the class of cases coming under the purview of the Act, of men who in part share in the proceeds of their female friends' traffic, must involve many instances in which no sane person—*i.e.* one who is not bitten by the rabid man-hatred of the Feminist and social purity monger—must regard the moral obliquity involved as not very serious. Take, for instance, the case of a man who is out of work, who is perhaps starving, and receives temporary assistance of this kind. Would any reasonable person allege that such a man was in the lowest depths of moral degradation, still less that he merited for this breach, at most, of fine delicacy of feeling, the flaying alive prescribed by the Act under consideration. Besides all this, it is well known that some women, shop assistants and others, gain part of their living by their reputable avocation and part in another way. Now presumably the handing over of a portion of her regular salary to her lover would not constitute the latter a flayable criminal, but the endowment of him with a portion of any of the "presents" obtained by her pursuit of her other calling would do so. The process of earmarking the permissible and the impermissible gift strikes one as very difficult even if possible.

The point last referred to leads us on to another reflection. If the man who "in whole or in part" lives on the proceeds of a woman's prostitution is of necessity a degraded wretch outside the pale of all humanity, as he is represented to be by the flogging fraternity, how about the employer or employeress of female labour who bases his or her scale of wages on the assumption that the girls and women he or she employs, supplement these wages by presents received after working hours, for their sexual favours— in other words, by prostitution? Many of these employers of labour are doubtless to be found among the noble band of advocates of White Slave Traffic Bills, flogging and social purity. The above persons, of course, are respectable members of society, while a *souteneur* is an outcast.

In addition to the motives before alluded to as actuating the promoters of the factitious and bogus so-called "White Slave" agitation, there is one very powerful political and economic motive which must not be left out of sight. In view of the existing "labour unrest," it is highly desirable from the point of view of our possessing and governing classes that popular attention should be drawn off labour wrongs and labour grievances on to something less harassing to the capitalist and official mind. Now the Anti-man agitation forms a capital red herring for drawing the popular scent off class opposition by substituting sex antagonism in its place.

If you can set public opinion off on the question of wicked Man and down-trodden Woman, you have done a good deal to help capitalistic enterprise to tide over the present crisis. The insistence of public opinion on better conditions for the labourer will thus be weakened by being diverted into urging forward vindictive laws against men, and for placing as far as may be the whole power of the State at the disposal of the virago, the shrew and the female sharper, in their designs upon their male victim. For, be it remembered, it is always the worst type of woman to whom the advantage of laws passed as the result of the Anti-man campaign accrues. The real nature of the campaign is crucially exhibited in some of the concrete demands put forward by its advocates.

One of the measures proposed in the so-called "Woman's Charter" drawn up with the approval of all prominent Feminists by Lady M'Laren (now Lady Aberconway) some four or five years back, and which had been previously advocated by other Feminist writers, was to the effect that a husband, in addition to his other liabilities, should be legally compelled to pay a certain sum to his wife, ostensibly as wages for her housekeeping services, no matter whether she performs the services well, or ill, or not at all. Whatever the woman is, or does, the husband has to pay all the same. Another of the clauses in this precious document is to the effect that a wife is to be under no obligation to follow her husband, compelled probably by the necessity of earning a livelihood for himself and her, to any place of residence outside the British Islands. That favourite crank of the Feminist, of raising the age of consent with the result of increasing the number of victims of the designing young female should speak for itself to every unbiassed person. One of the proposals which finds most favour with the Sentimental Feminist is the demand that in the case of the murder by a woman of her illegitimate child, the putative father should be placed in the dock as an accessory! In other words, a man should be punished for a crime of which he is wholly innocent, because the guilty person was forsooth a woman. That such a suggestion should be so much as entertained by otherwise sane persons is indeed significant of the degeneracy of mental and moral fibre induced by the Feminist movement, for it may be taken as typical. It reminds me of a Feminist friend of mine who, challenged by me, sought (for long in vain) to find a case in the courts in which a man was unduly favoured at the expense of a woman. At last he succeeded in lighting upon the following from somewhere in Scotland: A man and woman who had been drinking went home to bed, and the woman caused the death of her baby by "overlaying it." Both the man and the woman were brought before the court on the charge of manslaughter, for causing the death, by culpable negligence, of the infant. In accordance with the evidence, the woman who had overlaid the baby was convicted and sentenced to six months' imprisonment, and naturally the man, who had not done so, was released. Now, in the judgment of my Feminist friend, in other matters sane enough, the fact that the man who had not committed any offence was let off, while his female companion, who had, was punished, showed the bias of the court in favour of the man!! Surely this is a noteworthy illustration, glaring as it is, of how all judgment is completely overbalanced and destroyed in otherwise judicial minds—of how such minds are completely hypnotised by the adoption of the Feminist dogma. As a matter of fact, of course, the task my friend set himself to do was hopeless. As against the cases, which daily occur all over the country, of flagrant injustice to men and partiality to women on the part of the courts, there is, I venture to assert, not to be found a single case within the limits of the four seas of a judicial decision in the contrary sense—*i.e.* of one favouring the man at the expense of the woman.

This sex hatred, so often vindictive in its character, of men for men, which has for its results that "man-made" laws invariably favour the opposite sex, and that "man-administered justice" follows the same course, is a psychological problem which is well worth the earnest attention of students of sociology and thinkers generally.

CHAPTER IV
ALWAYS THE "INJURED INNOCENT"!

While what we have termed Political Feminism vehemently asserts its favourite dogma, the intellectual and moral equality of the sexes—that the woman is as good as the man if not better—Sentimental Feminism as vehemently seeks to exonerate every female criminal, and protests against any punishment being meted out to her approaching in severity that which would be awarded a man in a similar case. It does so on grounds which presuppose the old theory of the immeasurable inferiority, mental and moral, of woman, which are so indignantly spurned by every Political Feminist—*i.e.* in his or her capacity as such. We might suppose, therefore, that Political Feminism, with its theory of sex equality based on the assumption of equal sex capacity, would be in strong opposition in this matter with Sentimental Feminism, which seeks, as its name implies, to attenuate female responsibility on grounds which are not distinguishable from the old-fashioned assumption of inferiority. But does Political Feminism consistently adopt this logical position? Not one whit. It is quite true that some Feminists, when hard pressed, may grudgingly concede the untenability on rational grounds of the Sentimental Feminists' claims. But taken as a whole, and in their practical dealings, the Political Feminists are in accord with the Sentimental Feminists in claiming female immunity on the ground of sex. This is shown in every case where a female criminal receives more than a nominal sentence.

We have already given examples of the fact in question, and they could be indefinitely extended. At the end of the year 1911, at Birmingham, in the case of a woman convicted of the murder of her paramour by deliberately pouring inflammable oil over him while he was asleep, and then setting it afire, and afterwards not only exulting in the action but saying she was ready to do it again, the jury brought in recommendation to mercy with their verdict. And, needless to say, the influence of Political and Sentimental Feminism was too strong to allow the capital sentence to be carried out, even with such a fiendish wretch as this. In the case of the Italian woman in Canada, Napolitano, before mentioned, the female franchise societies issued a petition to Mr Borden, the Premier of Canada, in favour of the commutation of sentence. The usual course was adopted in this case, as in most others in which a woman murders a man—to wit, the truly "chivalrous" one of trying to blacken the character of the dead victim in defence of the action of the murderess. In other cases, more especially, of course, where the man is guilty of a crime against a woman, when mercy is asked for the offender, we are pitifully adjured to "think of the poor victim." As we have seen, Lord Haldane trotted out this exhortation in a case where it was absurdly inappropriate, since the much-commiserated "victim" had only herself to thank for being a "victim," and still more for remaining a "victim." We never hear this plea for the "victim" urged where the "victim" happens to be a man and the offender a woman. Compare this with the case of the boy of nineteen, Beal, whom Mr M'Kenna hanged for the murder of his sweetheart, and that in the teeth of an explanation given in the defence which was at least possible, if not probable, and which certainly, putting it at the very lowest, introduced an element of doubt into the case. Fancy a girl of nineteen being convicted, whatever the evidence, of having poisoned her paramour or even if, *per impossibile*, she were convicted, fancy her being given more than a short term of imprisonment! A man murdered by a woman is always the horrid brute, while the woman murdered by the man is just as surely the angelic victim. Anyone who reads reports of cases with an unbiassed mind must admit the absolute accuracy of this statement.

Divine woman is always the "injured innocent," not only in the graver crimes, such as murder, but also in the minor offences coming under the cognisance of the law. At the Ledbury Petty Sessions a woman in the employment of a draper, who had purloined goods to the amount of £150, was acquitted on the ground of "kleptomania," and this notwithstanding the fact that she had been in the employment of the prosecutor for over five years, had never complained of illness and had never been absent from business; also that her landlady gave evidence showing that she was sound in mind and body. At the very same sessions two men were sentenced respectively to eight and twelve months' imprisonment for stealing goods to the value of £5! (*John Bull*, 12th November 1910).

At this point I may be permitted to quote from the article formerly alluded to (*Fortnightly Review*, November 1911, case taken from a report in *The News of the World* of 28th February 1909): "A young woman shot at the local postman with a revolver; the bullet grazed his face, she having fired point blank at his head. Jury returned a verdict of not guilty, although the revolver was found on her when arrested, and the facts were admitted and were as follows:—At noon she left her house, crossing three fields to the house of the victim, who was at home and alone; upon his appearing she fired point blank at his head; he banged to the door, and thus turned off the bullet, which grazed his face and 'ploughed a furrow through his hair.' She had by her when arrested a revolver cocked and with four chambers undischarged."

Let us now take the crime of violent assault with attempt to do bodily injury. The following cases will serve as illustrative examples:—From *The News of the World*, 9th May 1909: A nurse in Belfast sued her lost swain for breach of promise. *She obtained £100 damages although it was admitted by her counsel that she had thrown vitriol over the defendant, thereby injuring him, and the defendant had not prosecuted her!* Also it was admitted that she had been "carrying on" with another man. From *The Morning Leader* of 8th July 1905 I have taken the following extraordinary facts as to the varied punishment awarded in cases of vitriol-throwing: That of a woman who threw vitriol over a sergeant at Aldershot, and was sentenced to six months' imprisonment without hard labour while a man who threw it over a woman at Portsmouth was tried and convicted at the Hants Assizes, on 7th July 1905, and sentenced by Mr Justice Bigham to twelve years' penal servitude! As regards the first case it will be observed that, (notwithstanding a crime, which in the case of a man was described by the judge as "cowardly and vile" and meriting twelve years' penal servitude) the woman was rewarded by damages for £100, to be obtained from the very victim whom she had done her best to maim for life (besides being unfaithful to him) and who had generously abstained from prosecuting.

But it is not merely in cases of murder, attempted murder or serious assault that justice is mocked by the present state of our law and its administration in the interests of the female sex. The same attitude is observed, the same farcical sentences on women, whether the crime be theft, fraud, common assault, criminal slander or other minor offences. We have the same preposterous excuses admitted, the same preposterous pleas allowed, and the same farcical sentences passed—if, indeed, any sentence be passed at all. The following examples I have culled at random:—From

John Bull, 26th February 1910: At the London Sessions, Mr Robert Wallace had to deal with the case of a well-dressed woman living at Hampstead, who pleaded guilty to obtaining goods to the amount of £50 by false pretences. In explanation of her crime it was stated that she was under a mistaken impression that her engagement would not lead to marriage, that she became depressed, and that she "did not know what she said or did," while in mitigation of punishment it was urged that the money had been repaid, that her fiancé could not marry her if she were sent to gaol, and that her life would be irretrievably ruined, and she was discharged! From *The Birmingham Post,* 4th February 1902: A female clerk (twenty-six) pleaded guilty to embezzling £5, 1s. 9d. on 16th November, £2, 2s. 4d. on 21st December and £5, 0s. 9d. on 23rd December last, the moneys of her employer. Prosecuting counsel said prisoner entered prosecutor's employ in 1900, and in June last her salary was raised to 27s. 6d. a week. The defalcations, which began a month before the increase, amounted to £134. She had falsified the books, and when suspicion fell upon her destroyed two books, in order, as she thought, to prevent detection. Her counsel pleaded for leniency on the ground of her previous good character *and because she was engaged*! The recorder merely bound her over, stating that her parents and young man were respectable, and so was the house in which she lodged! A correspondent mentions in *The Birmingham Post* of February 1902 a case where a woman had burned her employer's outhouses and property, doing £1800 worth of damage, and got off with a month's imprisonment. On the other hand, the *same* judge, at the *same* Quarter Sessions, thus dealt with two male embezzlers: C. C. (twenty-eight), clerk, who pleaded guilty to embezzling two sums of money from his master in August and September of 1901 (amounts not given), was sent to gaol for six calendar months; and S. G. (twenty-four), clerk, pleaded guilty to embezzling 7s. 6d. and 3s. For the defence it was urged that the prisoner had been poorly paid, and the recorder, hearing that a gentleman was prepared to employ the man as soon as released, sentenced him to three months' hard labour! O merciful recorder!

The "injured innocent" theory usually comes into play with magistrates when a woman is charged with aggravated annoyance and harassing of men in their business or profession, when, as already stated, the administrator of the law will usually tell the prosecutor that he cannot interfere. In the opposite case of a man annoying a woman under like circumstances he invariably has to find substantial sureties for his good behaviour or go to gaol. No injured innocence for him!

There is another case in which it seems probable that, animated by the same fixed idea, those responsible for the framing of laws have flagrantly neglected an obvious measure for public safety. We refer to the unrestricted sale of sulphuric acid (vitriol) which is permitted. Now here we have a substance subserving only very special purposes in industry, none in household economy, or in other departments, save for criminal ends, which is nevertheless procurable without let or hindrance. Is it possible to believe that this would be the case if men were in the habit of using this substance in settling their differences with each other, even still more if they employed it by way of emphasising their disapproval of the jilting of sweethearts? That it should be employed by women in wreaking their vengeance on recalcitrant lovers seems a natural if not precisely a commendable action, in the eyes of a Sentimental Feminist public opinion, and one which, on the mildest hypothesis, "doesn't matter." Hence a deadly substance may be freely bought and sold as though it were cod-liver oil. A very nice thing for dastardly viragoes for whom public opinion has only the mildest of censures! In any reasonable society the indiscriminate sale of corrosive substances would in itself be a crime punishable with a heavy term of imprisonment.

It is not only by men, and by a morbid public opinion inflamed by Feminist sentiment in general, that female criminals are surrounded by a halo of injured innocence. The reader can hardly fail to notice that such women have the effrontery to pretend to regard themselves in this light. This is often so in cases of assault, murder or attempted murder of lovers by their sweethearts. Such is, of course, particularly noticeable in the senselessly wicked outrages, of which more anon. The late Otto Weininger, in his book before quoted, "Geschlecht und Charakter" (Sex and Character), has some noteworthy remarks on this, remarks which, whether we accept his suggested theory or not, might well have been written as a comment on recent cases of suffragette crimes and criminals. "The male criminal," says Weininger, "has from his birth the same relation to the idea of value [moral value] as any other man in whom the criminal tendencies governing himself may be wholly absent. The female on the other hand often claims to be fully justified when she has committed the greatest conceivable infamy. While the genuine criminal is obtusely silent against all reproaches, a woman will express her astonishment and indignation that anyone can doubt her perfect right to act as she has done. Women are convinced of their being in the right without ever having sat in judgment on themselves. The male criminal, it may be true, does not do so either, but then he never maintains that he is in the right. He rather goes hastily out of the way of discussing right and wrong, because it reminds him of his guilt. In this fact we have a proof that he has a relationship to the [moral] idea, and that it is unfaithfulness to his better self of which he is unwilling to be reminded. No male criminal has ever really believed that injustice has been done him by punishment. The female criminal on the other hand is convinced of the maliciousness of her accusers, and if she is unwilling no man can persuade her that she has done wrong. Should someone admonish her, it is true that she often bursts into tears, begs for forgiveness and admits her fault; she may even believe indeed that she really feels this fault. Such is only the case, however, when she has felt inclined to do so, for this very dissolving in tears affects her always with a certain voluptuous pleasure. The male criminal is obstinate, he does not allow himself to be turned round in a moment as the apparent defiance of a woman may be converted into an apparent sense of guilt, where, that is, the accuser understands how to handle her" ("Geschlecht und Charakter," pp. 253-254). Weininger's conclusion is: "Not that woman is naturally evil or *anti*-moral, but rather that she is merely *a*-moral, in other words that she is destitute of what is commonly called 'moral sense.'" The cases of female penitents and others which seem to contradict this announcement Weininger explains by the hypothesis that "it is only in company and under external influence that woman can feel remorse."

Be all this as it may, the fact remains that women when most patently and obviously guilty of vile and criminal actions will, with the most complete nonchalance, insist that they are in the right. This may be, and very possibly often is, mere impudent effrontery, relying on the privilege of the female sex, or it may, in part at least, as Weininger insists, be traceable to "special deep-lying sex-characteristics." But in any case the singular fact is that men, and men even of otherwise judicial capacity, are to be found who are prepared virtually to accept the justice of this attitude, and who are ready to condone, if not directly to defend, any conduct, no matter how vile or how criminal, on the part of a woman. We have illustrations of this class of judgment almost every day, but I propose to give two instances of what I should deem typical, if slightly extreme, perversions of moral judgment on the part of two men, both of them of social and intellectual standing, and without any doubt personally of the highest integrity. Dr James Donaldson, Principal of the University of St Andrews, in his work entitled "Woman, her Position and Influence in Ancient Greece and Rome and among the Early Christians," commenting on the well-known story attributed to the year 331 B.C., which may or may not be historical, of the wholesale poisoning of their husbands by Roman matrons, as well as of subsequent cases of the same crime, concludes his remarks with these words: "It seems to me that we must regard them [namely these stories or facts, as we may choose to consider them] as indicating that the Roman matrons felt sometimes that they were badly treated, that they ought not to endure the bad treatment, and that they ought to take the only means that they possessed of expressing their feelings, and of wreaking vengeance, by employing poison" (p. 92). Now though it may be said that in this passage we have no direct justification of the atrocious crime attributed to the Roman matrons, yet it can hardly be denied that we have here a distinct condonation of the infamous and dastardly act, such a condonation as the worthy Principal of St Andrews University would hardly have meted out to men under any circumstances. Probably Professor Donaldson, in writing the above, felt that his comments would not be resented very strongly, even if not actually approved, by public opinion, steeped as it is at the present time in Feminism, political and sentimental.

Another instance, this time of direct special pleading to prove a woman guilty of an atrocious crime to be an "injured innocent." It is taken from an eminent Swiss alienist in his work on Sex. Dr Forel maintains a thesis which may or may not be true to the effect that the natural maternal instinct is either absent or materially weakened in the case of a woman who has given birth to a child begotten by rape, or under circumstances bordering upon rape, and indeed more or less in all cases where the woman is an unwilling participant in the sexual act. By way of illustration of this theory he cites the case of a barmaid in St Gallen who was seduced by her employer under such circumstances as those above mentioned; a child resulted, who was put out to nurse at an institution until five years of age, when it was handed over to the care of the mother. Now what does the woman do? Within a few hours of receiving the little boy into her keeping she took him to a lonely place and deliberately strangled him, in consequence of which she was tried and condemned. Now Dr Forel, in his Feminist zeal, feels it incumbent upon him to try to whitewash this female monster by urging, on the basis of this theory, the excuse that under the circumstances of its conception one could not expect the mother to have the ordinary instincts of maternity as regards her child. The worthy doctor is apparently so blinded by his Feminist prejudices that (quite apart from the correctness or otherwise of his theory) he is oblivious of the absurd irrelevancy of his argument. What, we may justly ask, has the maternal instinct, or its absence, to do with the guilt of the murderess of a helpless child committed to her care? Who or what the child was is immaterial! That a humane and otherwise clear-headed man like Dr Forel could take a wretch of this description under his *ægis*, and still more that in doing so he should serve up such utterly illogical balderdash by way of argument, is only one more instance of how the most sane-thinking men are rendered fatuous by the glamour of Sentimental Feminism.

In the present chapter we have given a few typical instances of the practice which constitutes one of the most conspicuous features of Modern Feminism and of the public opinion which it has engendered. We hear and read, *ad nauseam*, of excuses, and condonation, for every crime committed by a woman, while a crime of precisely similar a character and under precisely similar circumstances, where a man is the perpetrator, meets with nothing but virulent execration from that truculent ass, British public opinion, as manipulated by the Feminist fraternity, male and female. This state of public opinion reacts, of course, upon the tribunals and has the result that women are practically free to commit any offence they please, with always a splendid sporting chance of getting acquitted altogether, and a practical certainty that even if convicted they will receive farcical sentences, or, should the sentence be in any degree adequate to the offence, that such sentence will not be carried out. The way in which criminal law is made a jest and a mockery as regards female prisoners, the treatment of criminal suffragettes, is there in evidence. The excuse of health being endangered by their going without their breakfasts has resulted in the release after a few days of women guilty of the vilest crimes—*e.g.* the attempt to set fire to the theatre at Dublin. It may be well to recall the outrageous facts of modern female immunity and free defiance of the law as illustrated by one quotation of a description of the merry time of the window-smashers of March 1912 in Holloway prison given by a correspondent of *The Daily Telegraph*. The correspondent of that journal describes his visit to the aforesaid prison, where he said there appeared to have been no punishment of any kind for any sort of misbehaviour. "All over the place," he writes, "is noise—women calling to women everywhere, and the officials seem powerless to preserve even the semblance of discipline. A suffragist will call out her name while in a cell, and another one who knows her will answer, giving her name in return, and a conversation will then be carried on between the two. This chattering obtains all day and far into the night. The 'officials' as the wardresses prefer themselves called, have already given the prison the name of 'the monkey-house.' Certain it is that the prisoners are treated with all deference, the reason being perhaps that the number of officials is insufficient to establish proper order. While I was waiting yesterday one lady drove up in a carriage and pair, in which were two policemen and several bundles of clothes, to enter upon her sentence and this is the note which seems to dominate the whole of the prison. Seventy-six of the prisoners are supposed to be serving sentences with hard labour, but none of them are wearing prison clothes, and in only one or two instances have any tasks of any description been given, those generally being a little sewing or knitting." Again a member of the Women's Freedom League at a meeting on 19th May 1912 boasted that the suffragettes had a wing of their own at Holloway. "They had nice hot water pipes and all the latest improvements and were able to climb up to the window and exchange sentiments with their friends." She had saved money and enjoyed herself very much!!

Here we have a picture of the way the modern authorities of the law recognise the "injured innocence" of female delinquents who claim the right wantonly to destroy property. Our present society, based as it is on private property-holding, and which usually punished with the utmost severity any breach of the sanctity of private property, waives its claims where women are concerned. Similarly arson under circumstances directly endangering human life, for which the law prescribes the maximum sentence of penal servitude for life, is considered adequately punished by a week or two's imprisonment when those convicted of the crime are of the female sex. Oh, but they were acting from political motives! Good, and have not terrorist anarchists, Fenians and Irish dynamiters of the Land League days also acted from political motives? The terrorist anarchist, foolish and indefensible though his tactics may be, believes honestly enough that he is paving the way for the abolition of poverty, misery and social injustice, a far more vital thing than the franchise! The Irish Fenians and dynamiters pursued a similar policy and there is no reason to doubt their honest belief that it would further the cause of the freedom and national independence of Ireland. Yet were these "political" offenders dealt with otherwise than as ordinary criminals when convicted of acts qualified by the law as felonies? And their acts, moreover, whatever we may think of them otherwise, were, in most cases at least, politically logical from their own point of view, and not senseless injuries to unoffending persons, as those of the present-day female seekers after the suffrage.

CHAPTER V
THE "CHIVALRY" FAKE

The justification for the whole movement of Modern Feminism in one of its main practical aspects—namely, the placing of the female sex in the position of privilege, advantage and immunity—is concentrated in the current conception of "chivalry." It behoves us, therefore, to devote some consideration to the meaning and implication of this notion. Now this word chivalry is the *dernier ressort* of those at a loss for a justification of the modern privileging of women. But those who use it seldom give themselves the trouble to analyse the connotation of this term. Brought to book as to its meaning, most persons would probably define it as deference to, or consideration for, weakness, especially bodily weakness. Used in this sense, however, the term covers a very much wider ground than the "kow-towing" to the female section of the human race, usually associated with it. Boys, men whose muscular strength is below the average, domestic animals, etc., might all claim this special protection as a plea of chivalry, in their favour. And yet we do not find different criminal laws, or different rules of prison treatment, say, for men whose stamina is below the average. Neither do we find such men or boys exempted by law from corporal punishment in consequence of their weakness, unless as an exception in individual cases when the weakness amounts to dangerous physical disability. Neither, again, in the general affairs of life are we accustomed to see any such deference to men of weaker muscular or constitutional development as custom exacts in the case of women. Once more, looking at the question from the other side, do we find the claim of chivalry dropped in the case of the powerful virago or the muscularly developed female athlete, the sportswoman who rides, hunts, plays cricket, football, golf and other masculine games, and who may even fence or box? Not one whit!

It would seem then that the definition of the term under consideration, based on the notion of deference to mere weakness as such, will hardly hold water, since in its application the question of sex always takes precedence of that of weakness. Let us try again! Abandoning for the moment the definition of chivalry as a consideration for weakness, considered *absolutely*, as we may term it, let us see whether the definition of consideration for *relative* defencelessness—*i.e.* defencelessness in a given situation—will coincide with the current usage of the word. But here again we are met with the fact that the man in the hands of the law—to wit, in the grip of the forces of the State, ay, even the strongest man, were he a very Hercules, is in as precisely as defenceless and helpless a position relative to those in whose power he finds himself, as the weakest woman would be in the like case, neither more nor less! And yet an enlightened and chivalrous public opinion tolerates the most fiendish barbarities and excogitated cruelties being perpetrated upon male convicts in our gaols, while it shudders with horror at the notion of female convicts being accorded any severity of punishment at all even for the same, or, for that matter, more heinous offences. A particularly crass and crucial illustration is that infamous piece of one-sided sex legislation which has already occupied our attention in the course of the present volume—to wit, the so-called "White Slave Traffic Act" 1912.

It is plain then that chivalry as understood in the present day really spells sex privilege and sex favouritism pure and simple, and that any attempts to define the term on a larger basis, or to give it a colourable rationality founded on fact, are simply subterfuges, conscious or unconscious, on the part of those who put them forward. The etymology of the word chivalry is well known and obvious enough. The term meant originally the virtues associated with knighthood considered as a whole, bravery even to the extent of reckless daring, loyalty to the chief or feudal superior, generosity to a fallen foe, general open-handedness, and open-heartedness, including, of course, the succour of the weak and the oppressed generally, *inter alia*, the female sex when in difficulties. It would be idle, of course, to insist upon the historical definition of the term. Language develops and words in course of time depart widely from their original connotation, so that etymology alone is seldom of much value in practically determining the definition of words in their application at the present day. But the fact is none the less worthy of note that only a fragment of the original connotation of the word chivalry is covered by the term as used in our time, and that even that fragment is torn from its original connection and is made to serve as a scarecrow in the field of public opinion to intimidate all who refuse to act upon, or who protest against, the privileges and immunities of the female sex.[101:1]

[101:1] One among many apposite cases, which has occurred recently, was protested against in a letter to *The Daily Telegraph*, 21st March 1913, in which it was pointed out that while a suffragette got a few months' imprisonment in the second division for wilfully setting fire to the pavilion in Kew Gardens, a few days previously, at the Lewes Assizes, a man had been sentenced to five years' penal servitude for burning a rick!!

I have said that even that subsidiary element in the old original notion of chivalry which is now well-nigh the only surviving remnant of its original connotation is torn from its connection and hence has necessarily become radically changed in its meaning. From being part of a general code of manners enjoined upon a particular guild or profession it has been degraded to mean the exclusive right in one sex guaranteed by law and custom to certain advantages and exemptions without any corresponding responsibility. Let us make no mistake about this. When the limelight of a little plain but critical common-sense is turned upon this notion of chivalry hitherto regarded as so sacrosanct, it is seen to be but a poor thing after all; and when men have acquired the habit of habitually turning the light of such criticism upon it, the accusation, so terrible in the present state of public opinion, of being "unchivalrous" will lose its terrors for them. In the so-called ages of chivalry themselves it never meant, as it does to-day, the woman right or wrong. It never meant as it does to-day the general legal and social privilege of sex. It never meant a social defence or a legal exoneration for the bad and even the criminal woman, simply because she is a woman. It meant none of these things. All it meant was a voluntary or gratuitous personal service to the forlorn women which the members of the Knights' guild among other such services, many of them taking precedence of this one, were supposed to perform.

So far as courage is concerned, which was perhaps the first of the chivalric virtues in the old days, it certainly requires more courage in our days to deal severely with a woman when she deserves it (as a man would be dealt with in like circumstances) than it does to back up a woman against her wicked male opponent.

It is a cheap thing, for example, in the case of a man and woman quarrelling in the street, to play out the stage rôle of the bold and gallant

Englishman "who won't see a woman maltreated and put upon, not he!" and this, of course, without any inquiry into the merits of the quarrel. To swim with the stream, to make a pretence of boldness and bravery, when all the time you know you have the backing of conventional public opinion and mob-force behind you, is the cheapest of mock heroics.

Chivalry to-day means the woman, right or wrong, just as patriotism to-day means "my country right or wrong." In other words, chivalry to-day is only another name for Sentimental Feminism. Every outrageous pretension of Sentimental Feminism can be justified by the appeal to chivalry, which amounts (to use the German expression) to an "appeal from Pontius to Pilate." This Sentimental Feminism commonly called chivalry is sometimes impudently dubbed by its votaries, "manliness." It will presumably continue in its practical effects until a sufficient minority of sensible men will have the moral courage to beard a Feminist public opinion and shed a little of this sort of "manliness." The plucky Welshmen at Llandystwmdwy in their dealings with the suffragette rowdies on a memorable occasion showed themselves capable of doing this. In fact one good effect generally of militant suffragetteism seems to be the weakening of the notion of chivalry —*i.e.* in its modern sense of Sentimental Feminism—amongst the populace of this country.

The combination of Sentimental Feminism with its invocation of the old-world sentiment of chivalry which was based essentially on the assumption of the mental, moral and physical inferiority of woman to man, for its justification, with the pretensions of modern Political Feminism, is simply grotesque in its inconsistent absurdity. In this way Modern Feminism would fain achieve the feat of eating its cake and having it too. When political and economic rights are in question, *bien entendu*, such as involve gain and social standing, the assumption of inferiority magically disappears before the strident assertion of the dogma of the equality of woman with man—her mental and moral equality certainly! When, however, the question is of a different character—for example, for the relieving of some vile female criminal of the penalty of her misdeeds—then Sentimental Feminism comes into play, then the whole *plaidoyer* is based on the chivalric sentiment of deference and consideration for poor, weak woman. I may point out that here, if it be in the least degree logical, the plea for mercy or immunity can hardly be based on any other consideration than that of an intrinsic moral weakness in view of which the offence is to be condoned. The plea of physical weakness, if such be entertained, is here in most cases purely irrelevant. Thus, as regards the commutation of the death sentence, the question of the muscular strength or weakness of the condemned person does not come in at all. The same applies, *mutatis mutandis*, to many other forms of criminal punishment. But it must not be forgotten that there are two aspects of physical strength or weakness. There is, as we have already pointed out, the muscular aspect and the constitutional aspect. If we concede the female sex as essentially and inherently weaker in muscular power and development than the male, this by no means involves the assumption that woman is constitutionally weaker than man. On the contrary, it is a known fact attested, as far as I am aware, by all physiologists, no less than by common observation, that the constitutional toughness and power of endurance of woman in general far exceeds that of man, as explained in an earlier chapter. This resilient power of the system, its capacity for enduring strain, it may here be remarked in passing, is by no means necessarily a characteristic of a specially high stage of organic evolution. We find it indeed in many orders of invertebrate animals in striking forms. Be this as it may, however, the existence of this greater constitutional strength or resistant power in the female than in the male organic system—as crucially instanced by the markedly greater death-rate of boys than of girls in infancy and early childhood—should, in respect of severity of punishment, prison treatment, etc., be a strong counter-argument against the plea for leniency, or immunity in the case of female criminals, made by the advocates of Sentimental Feminism.

But these considerations afford only one more illustration of the utter irrationality of the whole movement of Sentimental Feminism identified with the notion of "chivalry." For the rest, we may find illustrations of this galore. A very flagrant case is that infamous "rule of the sea" which came so much into prominence at the time of the *Titanic* disaster. According to this preposterous "chivalric" Feminism, in the case of a ship foundering, it is the unwritten law of the seas, not that the passengers shall leave the ship and be rescued in their order as they come, but that the whole female portion shall have the right of being rescued before any man is allowed to leave the ship. Now this abominable piece of sex favouritism, on the face of it, cries aloud in its irrational injustice. Here is no question of bodily strength or weakness, either muscular or constitutional. In this respect, for the nonce, all are on a level. But it is a case of life itself. A number of poor wretches are doomed to a watery grave, simply and solely because they have not had the luck to be born of the privileged female sex.

Such is "chivalry" as understood to-day—the deprivation, the robbery from men of the most elementary personal rights in order to endow women with privileges at the expense of men. During the ages of chivalry and for long after it was not so. Law and custom then was the same for men as for women in its incidence. To quote the familiar proverb in a slightly altered form, *then*—"what was sauce for the gander was sauce for the goose." Not until the nineteenth century did this state of things change. Then for the first time the law began to respect persons and to distinguish in favour of sex.

Even taking the matter on the conventional ground of weakness and granting, for the sake of argument, the relative muscular weakness of the female as ground for her being allowed the immunity claimed by Modern Feminists of the sentimental school, the distinction is altogether lost sight of between weakness as such and *aggressive* weakness. Now I submit there is a very considerable difference between what is due to weakness that is harmless and unprovocative, and weakness that is *aggressive*, still more when this aggressive weakness presumes on itself as weakness, and on the consideration extended to it, in order to become tyrannical and oppressive. Weakness as such assuredly deserves all consideration, but aggressive weakness deserves none save to be crushed beneath the iron heel of strength. Woman at the present day has been encouraged by a Feminist public opinion to become meanly aggressive under the protection of her weakness. She has been encouraged to forge her gift of weakness into a weapon of tyranny against man, unwitting that in so doing she has deprived her weakness of all just claim to consideration or even to toleration.

CHAPTER VI
SOME FEMINIST LIES AND FALLACIES

By Feminist lies I understand false statements put forward by persons, many of whom should be perfectly well aware that they are false, apparently with the deliberate intention of misleading public opinion as to the real position of woman before the law. By fallacies I understand statements doubtless dictated by Feminist prepossessions or Feminist bias, but not necessarily suggesting conscious or deliberate *mala fides*.

Of the first order, the statements are made apparently with intentional dishonesty in so far as many of the persons making them are concerned, since we may reasonably suppose them to have intelligence and knowledge enough to be aware that they are contrary to fact. The talk about the wife being a chattel, for example, is so palpably absurd in the face of the existing law that it is nowadays scarcely worth making (although we do hear it occasionally even now). But it was not even true under the old common law of England, which, for certain disabilities on the one hand, conceded to the wife certain corresponding privileges on the other. The law of husband and wife, as modified by statute in the course of the nineteenth century, as I have often enough had occasion to point out, is a monument of legalised tyranny over the husband in the interests of the wife.

If in the face of the facts the word chattel, as applied to the wife, has become a little too preposterous even for Feminist controversial methods, there is another falsehood scarcely less brazen that we hear from Feminist fanatics every day. The wife, we are told, is the only *unpaid servant*! A more blatant lie could scarcely be imagined. As every educated person possessing the slightest acquaintance with the laws of England knows, the law requires the husband to maintain his wife in a manner according with his own social position; has, in other words, to feed, clothe and afford her all reasonable luxuries, which the law, with a view to the economic standing of the husband, regards as necessaries. This although the husband has no claim on the wife's property or income, however wealthy she may be. Furthermore, it need scarcely be said, a servant who is inefficient, lazy, or otherwise intolerable, can be dismissed or her wage can be lowered. Not so that privileged person, the legally wedded wife. It matters not whether she perform her duties well, badly, indifferently, or not at all, the husband's legal obligations remain just the same. It will be seen, therefore, that the wife in any case receives from the husband economic advantages compared with which the wages of the most highly paid servant in existence are a mere pauper's pittance. This talk we hear *ad nauseam*, from the Feminist side, of the wife being an "unpaid servant," is typical of the whole Feminist agitation. We find the same deliberate and unscrupulous dishonesty characterising it throughout. Facts are not merely perverted or exaggerated, they are simply turned upside down.

Another statement commonly made is that women's lower wages as compared with men's is the result of not possessing the parliamentary franchise. Now this statement, though not perhaps bearing on its face the wilful deception characterising the one just mentioned, is not any the less a perversion of economic fact, and we can hardly regard it otherwise than as intentional. It is quite clear that up to date the wages of men have not been raised by legislation, and yet sections of the working classes have possessed the franchise at least since 1867. What legislation has done for the men has been simply to remove obstacles in the way of industrial organisation on the part of the workman in freeing the trade unions from disabilities, and even this was begun, owing to working-class pressure from outside, long before —as long ago as the twenties of the last century under the auspices of Joseph Hume and Francis Place. Now women's unions enjoy precisely the same freedom as men's unions, and nothing stands in the way of working women organising and agitating for higher wages. Those who talk of the franchise as being necessary for working women in order to obtain equal industrial and economic advantages with working men must realise perfectly well that they are performing the oratorical operation colloquially known as "talking through their hat." The reasons why the wages of women workers are lower than those of men, whatever else may be their grounds, and these are, I think, pretty obvious, clearly are not traceable to anything which the concession of the franchise would remove. If it be suggested that a law could be enacted compulsorily enforcing equal rates of payment for women as for men, what the result would be the merest tyro in such matters can foresee—to wit, that it would mean the wholesale displacement of female by male labour over large branches of industry, and this, we imagine, is not precisely what the advocates of female suffrage are desirous of effecting.

Male labour, owing to its greater efficiency and other causes, being generally preferred by employers to female labour, it is not likely that, even for the sake of female *beaux yeux*, they are going to accept female labour in the place of male, on an equal wage basis. All this, of course, is quite apart from the question referred to on a previous page, as to the economic responsibilities in the interests of women, which our Feminist law-makers have saddled on the man—namely, the responsibility of the husband, and the husband alone, for the maintenance of his wife and family, obligations from anything corresponding to which the female sex is wholly free.

In a leaflet issued by the "Men's Federation for Women's Suffrage" it is affirmed that "many laws are on the statute book which inflict injustice on Women." We challenge this statement as an unmitigated falsehood. Its makers ought to know perfectly well that they cannot justify it. There are no laws on the statute book inflicting injustice on women as a Sex, but there are many laws inflicting injustice on men in the supposed interests of women. The worn-out tag which has so long done duty with Feminists in this connection—viz. the rule of the Divorce Court, that in order to procure divorce a wife has to prove cruelty as well as adultery on the part of a husband, whereas a husband has to prove adultery alone on the part of a wife—has already been dealt with and its rottenness as a specimen of a grievance sufficiently exposed in this work and elsewhere by the present writer. Is what the authors of the leaflet may possibly have in their mind (if they have anything at all) when they talk about statutes inflicting injustice on women, that the law does not carry sex vindictiveness against men far enough to please them? With all its flogging, penal servitude, hard labour and the rest, for offences against women, some of them of a comparatively trivial kind, does the law as regards severity on men not even yet satisfy the ferocious Feminist souls of the members of the "Men's Federation for Women's Suffrage"? This is the only explanation of the statement in question other than that it is sheer bald bluff designed to mislead those ignorant of the law.

Another flagrant falsehood perpetually being dinned into our ears by the suffragists is the statement that *women have to obey the same laws as men.* The conclusion drawn from this false statement is, of course, that since they have to obey these laws equally with men, they have an equal claim with men to take part in the making or the modifying of them. Now without pausing to consider the fallacy underlying the conclusion, we would point out that it is sufficient for our present purpose to call attention to the falsity of the initial assumption itself. It needs only one who follows current events and reads his newspaper with impartial mind to see that to allege that women *have to*, in the true sense of the words (*i.e.* are compelled to), obey the same laws as men is a glaringly mendacious statement. It is unnecessary in this place to go over once more the mass of evidence comprised in previous writings of my own—*e.g.* in the pamphlet, "The Legal Subjection of Man" (Twentieth Century Press), in the article, "A Creature of Privilege" (*Fortnightly Review*, November 1911), and elsewhere in the present volume, illustrating the unquestionable fact that though in theory women may have to obey the law as men have, yet in practice they are absolved from all the more serious consequences men have to suffer when they disobey it. The treatment recently accorded to the suffragettes for crimes such as wilful damage and arson, not to speak of their previous prison treatment when convicted for obstruction, disturbance and minor police misdemeanours, is a proof, writ large, of the mendacity of the statement that women no less than men have to obey the laws of the country, so far, that is, as any real meaning is attached to this phrase.

Another suffragist lie which is invariably allowed to pass muster by default, save for an occasional protest by the present writer, is the assumption that the English law draws a distinction as regards prison treatment, etc., as between political and non-political offenders. Everyone with even the most elementary legal knowledge is aware that no such distinction has ever been recognised or suggested by the English law—at least until the prison ordinance made quite recently, expressly to please the suffragettes, by Mr Winston Churchill when Home Secretary. However desirable many may consider such a distinction to be, nothing is more indubitable than the fact that it has never previously obtained in the letter or practice of the law of England. And yet, without a word of contradiction from those who know better, arguments and protests galore have been fabricated on the suffragist side, based solely on this impudently false assumption.

Misdemeanours and crimes at common law, when wilfully committed, have in all countries always remained misdemeanours and crimes, whatever motive can be conveniently put forward to account for them. A political offence has always meant the expression of opinions or the advocacy of measures or acts (not of the nature of common law crimes) which are in contravention of the existing law—*e.g.* a "libel" on the constituted authorities of the State, or the forcible disregard of a law or police regulation in hindrance of the right of public speech or meeting. This is what is meant by political offence in any country recognising such as a special class of offence entitling those committing it to special treatment. This is so where the matter refers to the internal legislation of the country. Where the question of extradition comes in the definition of political offence is, of course, wider. Take the extreme case, that of the assassination of a ruler or functionary, especially in a despotic State, where free Press and the free expression of opinion generally do not exist. This is undoubtedly a political, not a common law offence, *in so far as other countries are concerned*, and hence the perpetrator of such a deed has the right to claim immunity, on this ground, from extradition. The position assumable is, that under despotic conditions the progressive man is at war with the despot and those exercising authority under him; therefore, in killing the despot or the repositories of despotic authority, he is striking directly at the enemy. It would, however, be absurd for the agent in a deed of this sort to expect special political treatment *within the jurisdiction of the State itself immediately concerned*. As a matter of fact he never does so. Fancy a Russian Nihilist, when brought to trial, whining that he is a political offender and hence to be exempted from all harsh treatment! No, the Nihilist has too much self-respect to make himself ridiculous in this way. Hardly even the maddest Terrorist Anarchist would make such a claim. For example, the French law recognises the distinction between political and common law offences. But for all this the *bande tragique*, Bonnot and his associates, did not receive any benefit from the distinction or even claim to do so, though otherwise they were loud enough in proclaiming the political motives inspiring them. Even as regards extradition, running amuck at large, setting fire promiscuously to private buildings or injuring the ordinary non-political citizen, as a "protest," would not legally come into the category of political offences and hence protect their authors from being surrendered as ordinary criminals.

The real fact, of course, is that all this talk on the part of suffragettes and their backers about "political" offences and "political" prison treatment is only a mean and underhand way of trying to secure special sex privileges under false pretences. Those who talk the loudest in the strain in question know this perfectly well.

These falsehoods are dangerous, in spite of what one would think ought to be their obvious character as such, by reason of the psychological fact that you only require to repeat a lie often enough, provided you are uncontradicted, in order for the aforesaid lie to be received as established truth by the mass of mankind ("mostly fools," as Carlyle had it).

It is a preposterous claim, I contend, that any misdemeanour and *a fortiori* any felony has, law apart, and even from a merely ethical point of view, any claim to special consideration and leniency on the bare declaration of the felon or misdemeanant that it had been dictated by political motive. In no country, at any time, has the mere assertion of political motive been held to bring an ordinary crime within the sphere of treatment of political offences. According to the legal and ethical logic of the suffragettes, it is perfectly open for them to set on fire theatres, churches and houses, and even to shoot down the harmless passer-by in the street, and claim the treatment of first-class misdemeanants on the ground that the act was done as a protest against some political grievance under which they imagined themselves to be labouring. The absurdity of the suggestion is evident on its mere statement. And yet the above preposterous assumption has been suffered equally with the one last noted to pass virtually without protest, and what is more serious, it has been acted upon by the authorities as though it were indubitably sound law as well as sound ethics! It may be pointed out that what has cost many an Irish Fenian in the old days, and many a Terrorist Anarchist at a later date, a sentence of penal servitude for life, can be indulged in by modern suffragettes at the expense of a few weeks' imprisonment in the first or second division. Of course, this whole talk of "political offences," when they are, on the face of them, mere common crimes, is purely and simply a trick designed to shield the cowardly and contemptible female creatures who perpetrate these senseless and dastardly outrages from the punishment they deserve and would receive if they had not the good fortune to be of the privileged sex. In the case of men this impudent nonsense would, of course, never have been put forward, and, if it had, would have been summarily laughed out of court. That it should be necessary to point out these things in so many words is a striking illustration of the moral and intellectual atrophy produced by Feminism in the public mind.

There is another falsehood we often hear by way of condoning the infamous outrages of the suffragettes. The excuse is often offered when the illogical pointlessness of the "militant" methods of the modern suffragette are in question: "Oh! men have also done the same things: men have used violence to attain political ends!" Now the fallacy involved in this retort is plain enough.

It may be perfectly true that men have used violence to attain their ends on occasion. But to assert this fact in the connection in question is purely irrelevant. There is violence *and* violence. It is absolutely false to say that men have ever adopted purposeless and inane violence *as a policy*. The violence of men has always had an intelligible relation to the ends they had in view, either proximate or ultimate. They pulled down Hyde Park railings in 1866. Good! But why was this? Because they wanted to hold a meeting, and found the park closed against them, the destruction of the railings being the only means of gaining access to the park. Again, the Reform Bill riots of 1831 were at least all directed against Government property and governmental persons—that is, the enemy with whom they were at war. In most cases, as at Bristol and Nottingham, there was (as in that of the Hyde Park railings) a very definite and immediate object in the violence and destruction committed—namely, the release of persons imprisoned for the part they had taken in the Reform movement, by the destruction of the gaols where they were confined. What conceivable analogy have these things with a policy of destroying private property, setting fire to tea pavilions, burning boat-builders' stock-in-trade, destroying private houses, poisoning pet dogs, upsetting jockeys, defacing people's correspondence, including the postal orders of the poor, mutilating books in a college library, pictures in a public gallery, etc., etc.? And all these, *bien entendu*, not openly and in course of a riot, but furtively, in the pursuit of a deliberately premeditated policy! Have, I ask, men ever, in the course of the world's history, committed mean, futile and dastardly crimes such as these in pursuit of any political or public end? There can be but one answer to this question. Every reader must know that there is no analogy whatever between suffragettes' "militancy" and the violence and crimes of which men may have been guilty. Even the Terrorist Anarchist, however wrong-headed he may be, and however much his deeds may be deemed morally reprehensible, is at least logical in his actions, in so far as the latter have always had some definite bearing on his political ends and were not mere senseless "running amuck." The utterly disconnected, meaningless and wanton character signalising the policy of the "militant" suffragettes would of itself suffice to furnish a conclusive argument for the incapacity of the female intellect to think logically or politically, and hence against the concession to women of public powers, political, judicial or otherwise.

Another fallacy analogous to the preceding, inasmuch as it seeks to counterbalance female defects and weaknesses by the false allegation of corresponding deficiencies in men, is the Feminist retort sometimes heard when the question of hysteria in women is raised: "Oh! men can also suffer from hysteria!" This has been already dealt with in an earlier chapter, but for the sake of completing the list of prominent Feminist fallacies I restate it concisely here. Now as we have seen it is exceedingly doubtful whether this statement is true in any sense whatever. There are eminent authorities who would deny that men ever have true hysteria. There are others, of course, again, who would extend the term hysteria so as to include every form of neurasthenic disturbance. The question is largely, with many persons who discuss the subject, one of terminology. It suffices here to cut short quibbling on this score. For the nonce, let us drop the word hysteria and formulate the matter as follows:—Women are frequently subject to a pathological mental condition, differing in different cases but offering certain well-marked features in common, a condition which seldom, if ever, occurs in men. This I take to be an incontrovertible proposition based upon experience which will be admitted by every impartial person.

Now the existence of the so-called hysterical man I have hitherto found to be attested on personal experience solely by certain Feminist medical practitioners who allege that they have met with him in their consulting-rooms. His existence is thus vouchsafed for just as the reality of the sea-serpent is vouchsafed for by certain sea captains or other ancient mariners. Far be it from me to impugn the ability, still less the integrity, of these worthy persons. But in either case I may have my doubts as to the accuracy of their observation or of their diagnosis. It may be that the sea-serpent exists and it may be that hysteria is at times discoverable in male persons. But while a conclusive proof of the discovery of a single sea-serpent of the orthodox pattern would go far to justify the yarn of the ancient mariner, the proof of the occurrence, in an occasional case, of hysteria in men, would not by far justify the implied contention that hysteria is not essentially a female malady. If hysterical men are as common a phenomenon as certain hard-pressed Feminists would make out, what I want to know is: Where are they? While we come upon symptoms which would be commonly attributed to hysteria in well-nigh every second or third woman of whose life we have any intimate knowledge, how often do we find in men symptoms in any way resembling these? In my own experience I have come across but two cases of men giving indications of a temperament in any way analogous to that of the "hysterical woman." After all, the experience of the average layman, and in this I contend my own is more or less typical, is more important in the case of a malady manifesting itself in symptoms obvious to common observation, such as the one we are considering, than that of the medical practitioner, who by reason of his profession would be especially likely to see cases, if there were any at all, however few they might be. The possibility, moreover, at least suggests itself, that the latter may often mistake for hysteria (using the word in the sense commonly applied to the symptoms presented by women) symptoms resulting from general neurasthenia or even from purely extraneous causes, such as alcohol, drugs, etc. That this is sometimes the case is hardly open to question. That the pathological mental symptoms referred to as prevalent in the female, whether we attribute them to hysteria or not, are rarely if ever found in the male sex is an undoubted fact. The rose, it is said, is as sweet by any other name, and whether we term these affections symptoms of hysteria, or describe them as hysteria itself, or deny that they have anything to go with "true hysteria," their existence and frequency in the female sex remains nevertheless a fact. No! whether some of the symptoms of hysteria, "true" or "so-called," are occasionally to be found in men or not, every impartial person must admit that they are extremely rare, whereas as regards certain pathological mental symptoms, common in women and popularly identified (rightly or wrongly) with hysteria, there is, I contend, little evidence of their occurring in men at all. Wriggle and prevaricate as they may, it is impossible for Suffragists and Feminists to successfully evade the undoubted truth that the mentality of women is characterised constitutionally by a general instability, manifesting itself in pathological symptoms radically differing in nature and in frequency from any that obtain in men.

Very conspicuous among the fallacies that have done yeoman service in the Feminist Movement is the assumption that women are constitutionally the "weaker sex." This has also been discussed by us in Chapter II., but the latter may again be supplemented here by a few further remarks, so deeply rooted is this fallacy in public opinion. The reason of the unquestioned acceptance of the assumption is partly due to a confusion of two things under one name. The terms, "bodily strength" and "bodily weakness" cover two distinct facts. The attribution of greater bodily weakness to the female sex than to the male undoubtedly expresses a truth, but no less does the attribution of greater bodily strength to the female than to the male sex equally express a truth. In size, weight and muscular development, average man has an unquestionable, and in most cases enormous, advantage over average woman. It is in this sense that the bodily structure of the human female can with some show of justice be described as frail. On the other hand, as regards tenacity of life, recuperative power and what we may term toughness of constitution, woman is without doubt considerably stronger than man. Now this vigour of constitution may, of course, also be described as bodily strength, and to this confusion the assumption of the general frailty of the female bodily organism as compared with the male has acquired general currency in the popular mind.

The most carefully controlled and reliable statistics of the Registrar-General and other sources show the enormously greater mortality of men than of women at all ages and under all conditions of life. Under the age of five the evidence shows that 120 boys die to every 100 girls. In adult life the Registrar-General shows that diseases of the chest are the cause of nearly 40 per cent. more deaths among men than among women. That violence and accident should be the occasion of 150 per cent. more deaths amongst men than women is accounted for, partly, at least, by the greater exposure of men, although the enormous disparity would lead one to suspect that here also the inferior resisting power in the male constitution plays a not inconsiderable part in the result. The report of the medical officer to the Local Government Board proves that between the ages of fifty-five and sixty-five there is a startling difference in numbers between the deaths of men and those of women. The details for the year 1910 are as follows:—

Diseases	Males	Females
Nervous system	1614	1240
Heart	5762	5336
Blood vessels	3424	3298
Respiratory system	3110	2473
Digestive system	1769	1681
Kidneys, etc.	2241	1488
Acute infections	2259	1164
Violent deaths	1624	436

Various additional causes, connected with the more active and anxious life of men, the greater strain to which they are subjected, their greater exposure alike to infection and to accident, may explain a certain percentage of the excessive death-rate of the male population as opposed to the female, yet these explanations, even allowing the utmost possible latitude to them, really only touch the fringe of the difference, with the single exception of deaths from violence and accident above alluded to, where liability and exposure may account for a somewhat larger percentage. The great cause of the discrepancy remains, without doubt, the enormously greater potentiality of resistance, in other words of constitutional strength, in the female bodily organism as compared with the male.

We must now deal at some length with a fallacy of some importance, owing to the apparatus of learning with which it has been set forth, to be found in Mr Lester F. Ward's book, entitled "Pure Sociology," notwithstanding that its fallacious nature is plain enough when analysed. Mr

Ward terms his speculation the "Gynœcocentric Theory," by which he understands apparently the Feminist dogma of the supreme importance of the female in the scheme of humanity and nature generally. His arguments are largely drawn from general biology, especially that of inferior organisms. He traces the various processes of reproduction in the lower departments of organic nature, subdivision, germination, budding, etc., up to the earlier forms of bi-sexuality, culminating in conjugation or true sexual union. His standpoint he thus states in the terms of biological origins: "Although reproduction and sex are two distinct things, and although a creature that reproduces without sex cannot properly be called either male or female, still so completely have these conceptions become blended in the popular mind that a creature which actually brings forth offspring out of its own body, is instinctively classed as female. The female is the fertile sex, and whatever is fertile is looked upon as female. Assuredly it would be absurd to look upon an organism propagating sexually as male. Biologists have proceeded from this popular standpoint and regularly speak of 'mother cells,' and 'daughter cells.' It, therefore, does no violence to language or to science to say that life begins with the female organism and is carried on a long distance by means of females alone. In all the different forms of a-sexual reproduction, from fission to parthenogenesis, the female may in this sense be said to exist alone and perform all the functions of life, including reproduction. In a word, life begins as female."

In the above remarks it will be seen that Mr Ward, so to say, jumps the claim of a-sexual organisms to be considered as female. This, in itself a somewhat questionable proceeding, serves him as a starting-point for his theory. The a-sexual female (?), he observes, is not only primarily the original sex, but continues throughout, the main trunk, though afterwards the male element is added "for the purposes of fertilisation." "Among millions of humble creatures," says Mr Ward, "the male is simply and solely a fertiliser." The writer goes on in his efforts to belittle the male sex in the sphere of biology. "The gigantic female spider and the tiny male fertiliser, the Mantis insect with its similarly large and ferocious female, bees, and mosquitoes," all are pressed into the service. Even the vegetable kingdom, in so far as it shows signs of sex differentiation, is brought into the lists in favour of his theory of female supremacy, or "gynœcocentricism," as he terms it.

This theory may be briefly stated as follows:—In the earliest organisms displaying sex differentiation, it is the female which represents the organism proper, the rudimentary male existing solely for the purpose of the fertilisation of the female. This applies to most of the lower forms of life in which the differentiation of sex obtains, and in many insects, the Mantis being one of the cases specially insisted upon by our author. The process of the development of the male sex is by means of the sexual selection of the female. From being a mere fertilising agent, gradually, as evolution proceeds, it assumes the form and characteristics of an independent organism like the original female trunk organism. But the latter continues to maintain its supremacy in the life of the species, by means chiefly of sexual selection, until the human period, *i.e.* more or less (!), for Mr Ward is bound to admit signs of male superiority in the higher vertebrates—viz. birds and mammals. This superiority manifests itself in size, strength, ornamentation, alertness, etc. But it is with man, with the advent of the reasoning faculty, and, as a consequence, of human supremacy, that it becomes first unmistakably manifest. This superiority, Mr Ward contends, has been developed under the ægis of the sexual selection of the female, and enabled cruel and wicked man to subject and enslave down-trodden and oppressed woman, who has thus been crushed by a Frankenstein of her own creation. Although in various earlier phases of human organisation woman still maintains her social supremacy, this state of affairs soon changes. Androcracy establishes itself, and woman is reduced to the rôle of breeding the race and of being the servant of man. Thus she has remained throughout the periods of the higher barbarism and of civilisation. Our author regards the lowest point of what he terms the degradation of woman to have been reached in the past, and the last two centuries as having witnessed a movement in the opposite direction—namely, towards the emancipation of woman and equality between the sexes. (*Cf.* "Pure Sociology," chap. xiv., and especially pp. 290-377.)

The above is a brief, but, I think, not unfair skeleton statement of the theory which Mr Lester Ward has elaborated in the work above referred to, in great detail and with immense wealth of illustration. But now I ask, granting the correctness of Mr Ward's biological premises and the accuracy of his exposition, and I am not specialist enough to be capable of criticising these in detail: What does it all amount to? The "business end" (as the

Americans would say) of the whole theory, it is quite evident, is to afford a plausible and scientific basis for the Modern Feminist Movement, and thus to further its practical pretensions. What Mr Ward terms the androcentric theory, at least as regards man and the higher vertebrates, which is on the face of it supported by the facts of human experience and has been accepted well-nigh unanimously up to quite recent times, is, according to him, all wrong. The male element in the universe of living things is not the element of primary importance, and the female element the secondary, but the converse is the case. For this contention Mr Ward, as already pointed out, has, by dint of his biological learning, succeeded at least in making out a case *in so far as lower forms of life are concerned.* He has, however, to admit—a fatal admission surely—that evolution has tended progressively to break down the superiority of the female (by means, as he contends, of her own sexual selection) and to transfer sex supremacy to the male, according to Mr Ward, hitherto a secondary being, and that this tendency becomes very obvious in most species of birds and mammals. With the rise of man, however, out of the *pithecanthropos*, the *homosynosis*, or by whatever other designation we may call the intermediate organism between the purely animal and the purely human, and the consequent supersession of instinct as the dominant form of intelligence by reason, the question of superiority, as Mr Ward candidly admits, is no longer doubtful, and upon the unquestionable superiority of the male, in due course of time, follows the unquestioned supremacy. It is clear then that, granting the biological premises of our author that the lowest sexual organisms are virtually female and that in the hermaphrodites the female element predominates; that in the earliest forms of bi-sexuality the fertilising or male element was merely an offshoot of the female trunk and that this offshoot develops, mainly by means of sexual selection on the part of the female, into an organism similar to the latter; that not until we reach the higher vertebrates, the birds and the mammals, do we find any traces of male superiority; and that this superiority only becomes definite and obvious, leading to male domination, in the human species—granting all this, I say, what argument can be founded upon it in support of the equal value physically, intellectually and morally of the female sex in human society, or the desirability of its possessing equal political power with men in such society? On the contrary, Mr Ward's whole exposition, with his biological facts of illustration, would seem to point rather in the opposite direction. We seem surely to have here, if Mr Ward's premises be accepted as to the primitive insignificance of the male element—at first overshadowed and dominated by the female stem, but gradually evolving in importance, character and fruition, till we arrive at man the highest product of evolution up to date—a powerful argument for anti-Feminism. On Mr Ward's own showing, we find that incontestible superiority, both in size and power of body and brain, has manifested itself in Androcracy, when the female is relegated, in the natural course of things, to the function of child-bearing. This, it can hardly be denied, is simply one more instance of the general process of evolution, whereby the higher being is evolved from the lower, at first weak and dependent upon its parent, the latter remaining dominant until the new being reaches maturity, when in its turn it becomes supreme, while that out of which it developed, and of which it was first the mere offshoot, falls into the background and becomes in its turn subordinate to its own product.

Let us turn now to another scientific fallacy, the result of a good man struggling with adversity—*i.e.* a sound and honest scientific investigator, but one who, at the same time, is either himself obsessed with the principles of Feminism as with a religious dogma, or else is nervously afraid of offending others who are. His attitude reminds one of nothing so much as that of the orthodox geologist of the first half of the nineteenth century, who wrote in mortal fear of incurring the *odium theologicum* by his exposition of the facts of geology, and who was therefore nervously anxious to persuade his readers that the facts in question did not clash with the Mosaic cosmogony as given in the Book of Genesis. With Mr Havelock Ellis in his work, "Man and Woman," it is not the dogma of Biblical infallibility that he is concerned to defend, but a more modern dogma, that of female equality, so dear to the heart of the Modern Feminist. Mr Ellis's efforts to evade the consequences of the scientific truths he honestly proclaims are almost pathetic. One cannot help noticing, after his exposition of some fact that goes dead against the sex-equality theory as contended for by Feminists, the eagerness with which he hastens to add some qualifying statement tending to show that after all it is not so incompatible with the Feminist dogma as it might appear at first sight.

The *pièce de résistance*, however, of Mr Havelock Ellis is contained in his "conclusion." The author has for his problem to get over the obvious incompatibility of the truth he has himself abundantly demonstrated in the course of his book, that the woman-type, in every respect, physiological and psychological, approaches the child-type, while the man-type, in its proper progress towards maturity, increasingly diverges from it. The obvious implication of this fact is surely plain, on the principle of the development of the individual being a shorthand reproduction of the evolution of the species, or, to express it in scientific phraseology, of *ontogeny* being the abbreviated recapitulation of the stages presented by *philogeny*. If we proceed on this well-accredited and otherwise universally accepted principle of biology, the inference is clear enough—to wit, that woman is, as Herbert Spencer and others have pointed out, simply "undeveloped man"—in other words, that Woman represents a lower stage of evolution than Man. Now this would obviously not at all suit the book of Mr Ellis's Feminism. Explained away it has to be in some fashion or other. So our author is driven to the daring expedient of throwing overboard one of the best established generalisations of modern biology, and boldly declaring that the principle contained therein is reversed (we suppose "for this occasion only") in the case of Man. In this way he is enabled to postulate a theory consoling to the Feminist soul, which affirms that adult man is nearer in point of development to his pre-human ancestor than either the child or the woman! The physiological and psychological analogies observable between the child and the savage, and even, especially in early childhood, between the child and the lower mammalian types—analogies which, notably in the life of instinct and passion, are traceable readily also in the human female—all these count for nothing; they are not dreamt of in Mr Ellis's Feminist philosophy. The Modern Feminist dogma requires that woman should be recognised as equal in every respect (except in muscular strength) with man, and if possible, as rather superior to him. If Nature has not worked on Feminist lines, as common observation and scientific research alike testify on the face of things, naughty Nature must be "corrected," in theory, at least, by the ingenuity of Feminist savants of the degraded male persuasion. To this end we must square our scientific hypotheses!

The startling theory of Mr Havelock Ellis, which must seem, one would think, to all impartial persons, so out of accord with all the acknowledged laws and facts of biological science, appears to the present writer, it must be confessed, the very *reductio ad absurdum* of Feminist controversial perversity.

I will conclude this chapter on Feminist Lies and Fallacies with a fallacy of false analogy or false illustration, according as we may choose to term it. This quasi-argument was recently put forward in a defence speech by one of the prisoners in a suffragette trial and was subsequently repeated by George Bernard Shaw in a letter to *The Times*. Put briefly, the point attempted to be made is as follows:—Apostrophising men, it is said: "How would you like it if the historical relations of the sexes were reversed, if the making and the administrating of the laws and the whole power of the State were in the hands of women? Would not you revolt in such a condition of affairs?" Now to this quasi-argument the reply is sufficiently clear. The moral intended to be conveyed in the hypothetical question put, is that women have just as much right to object to men's domination, as men would have to object to women's domination. But it is plain that the point of the whole question resides in a *petitio principie*—to wit, in the assumption that those challenged admit equal intellectual capacity and equal moral stability as between the average woman and the average man. Failing this assumption the challenge becomes senseless and futile. If we ignore mental and moral differences it is only a question of degree as to when we are landed in obvious absurdity. In "Gulliver's Travels" we have a picture of society in which horses ruled the roost, and lorded it over human beings. In this satire Swift in effect put the question: "How would you humans like to be treated by horses as inferiors, just as horses are treated by you to-day?" I am, be it remembered, not instituting any comparison between the two cases, beyond pointing out that the argument as an argument is intrinsically the same in both.

CHAPTER VII

THE PSYCHOLOGY OF THE MOVEMENT

We have already spoken of two strains in Modern Feminism which, although commonly found together, are nevertheless intrinsically distinguishable. The first I have termed Sentimental Feminism and the second Political Feminism. Sentimental Feminism is in the main an extension and emotional elaboration of the old notion of chivalry, a notion which in the period when it was supposed to have been at its zenith, certainly played a very much smaller part in human affairs than it does in its extended and metamorphosed form in the present day. We have already analysed in a former chapter the notion of chivalry. Taken in its most general and barest form it represents the consideration for weakness which is very apt to degenerate into a worship of mere weakness. *La faiblesse prime le droit* is not necessarily nearer justice than *la force prime le droit*; although to hear much of the talk in the present day one would imagine that the inherent right of the weak to oppress the strong were a first principle of eternal rectitude. But the theory of chivalry is scarcely invoked in the present day save in the interests of one particular form of weakness—viz. the woman as the muscularly weaker sex, and here it has acquired an utterly different character.[141:1]

[141:1] As regards this point it should be remarked that mediæval chivalry tolerated (as Wharton expressed it in his "History of Poetry") "the grossest indecencies and obscenities between the sexes," such things as modern puritanism would stigmatise with such words as "unchivalrous," "unmanly" and the like. The resemblance between the modern worship of women and the relations of the mediæval knight to the female sex is very thin indeed. Modern claims to immunity for women from the criminal law and mediæval chivalry are quite different things.

Chivalry, as understood by Modern Sentimental Feminism, means unlimited licence for women in their relations with men, and unlimited coercion for men in their relations with women. To men all duties and no rights, to women all rights and no duties, is the basic principle underlying Modern Feminism, Suffragism, and the bastard chivalry it is so fond of invoking. The most insistent female shrieker for equality between the sexes among Political Feminists, it is interesting to observe, will, in most cases, on occasion be found an equally insistent advocate of the claims of Sentimental Feminism, based on modern metamorphosed notions of chivalry. It never seems to strike anyone that the muscular weakness of woman has been forged by Modern Feminists into an abominable weapon of tyranny. Under cover of the notion of chivalry, as understood by Modern Feminism, Political and Sentimental Feminists alike would deprive men of the most elementary rights of self-defence against women and would exonerate the latter practically from all punishment for the most dastardly crimes against men. They know they can rely upon the support of the sentimental section of public opinion with some such parrot cry of "What! Hit a woman!"

Why not, if she molests you?

"Treat a woman in this way!" "Shame!" responds automatically the crowd of Sentimental Feminist idiots, oblivious of the fact that the real shame lies in their endorsement of an iniquitous sex privilege. If the same crowd were prepared to condemn any special form of punishment or mode of treatment as inhumane for both sexes alike, there would, of course, be nothing to be said. But it is not so. The most savage cruelty and vindictive animosity towards men leaves them comparatively cold, at most evoking a mild remonstrance as against the inflated manifestation of sentimental horror and frothy indignation produced by any slight hardship inflicted by way of punishment (let us say) on a female offender.

The psychology of Sentimental Feminism generally is intimately bound up with the curious phenomenon of the hatred of men by their own sex as such. With women, in spite of what is sometimes alleged, one does not find this phenomenon of anti-sex. On the contrary, nowadays we are in presence of a powerful female sex-solidarity indicating the beginnings of a strong sex-league of women against men. But with men, as already said, in all cases of conflict between the sexes, we are met with a callous indifference, alternating with positive hostility towards their fellow-men, which seems at times to kill in them all sense of justice. This is complemented on the other side by an imbecile softness towards the female sex in general which reminds one of nothing so much as of the maudlin *bonhomie* of the amiable drunkard. This besotted indulgence, as before noted, is proof even against the outraged sense of injury to property.

As we all know, offences against property, as a rule, are those the average bourgeois is least inclined to condone, yet we have recently seen a campaign of deliberate wanton destruction by arson and other means, directed expressly against private property, which nevertheless the respectable propertied bourgeois, the man of law and order, has taken pretty much "lying down." Let us suppose another case. Let us imagine an anarchist agitation, with a known centre and known leaders, a centre from which daily outrages were deliberately planned by these leaders and carried out by their emissaries, all, *bien entendu*, of the male persuasion.

Now what attitude does the reader suppose "public opinion" of the propertied classes would adopt towards the miscreants who were responsible for these acts? Can he not picture to himself the furious indignation, the rabid diatribes, the advocacy of hanging, flogging, penal servitude for life, as the minimum punishment, followed by panic legislation on these lines, which would ensue as a consequence. Yet of such threatenings and slaughter, where suffragettes who imitate the policy of the Terrorist Anarchist are concerned, we hear not a sound. The respectable propertied bourgeois, the man of law and order, will, it is true, probably condemn these outrages in an academic way, but there is an undernote of hesitancy which damps down the fire of his indignation. There is no vindictiveness, no note of atrocity in his expostulations; nay, he is even prepared, on occasion, to argue the question, while maintaining the impropriety, the foolishness, the "unwomanliness" of setting fire to empty houses, cutting up golf links, destroying correspondence, smashing windows and the like. But of fiery indignation, of lurid advocacy of barbaric punishments, or of ferocity in general, we have not a trace. On the contrary, a certain willingness to admit and even to emphasise the disinterestedness of these female criminals is observable. As regards this last point, we must again insist on what was pointed out on a previous page, that the disinterestedness and unselfishness of many a male bomb-throwing anarchist who has come in for the righteous bourgeois' sternest indignation, are, at least, as unquestionable as those of the female house-burners and window-smashers. Moreover the anarchist, however wrong-headed he may have been in his action, as once before remarked, it must not be forgotten, had at least for the goal of his endeavours, not merely the acquirement of a vote, but the revolution which he conceived would abolish human misery and raise humanity to a higher level.

In this strange phenomenon, therefore, in which the indignation of the bourgeois at the wanton and wilful violation of the sacredness of his idol, is reduced to mild remonstrance and its punitive action to a playful pretence, we have a crucial instance of the extraordinary influence of Feminism over the modern mind. That the propertied classes should take arson and wilful destruction of property in general, with such comparative equanimity because the culprits are women, acting in the assumed interest of a cause that aims at increasing the influence of women in the State, is the most striking illustration we can have of the power of Feminism. We have here a double phenomenon, the unreasoning hatred of man as a sex, by men, and their equally unreasoning indulgence towards the other sex. As we indicated above, not only is the sense of *esprit de corps* entirely absent among modern men as regards their own sex, while strongly present in modern women, but this negative characteristic has become positive on the other side. Thus the modern sex problem presents us with a reversal of the ordinary sociological law of the solidarity of those possessing common interests.

It remains to consider the psychological explanation of this fact. Why should men so conspicuously prefer the interests of women before those of their own sex? That this is the case with modern man the history of the legislation of the last fifty years shows, and the undoubted fact may be found further illustrated in the newspaper reports of well-nigh every trial, whether at civil or criminal law, quite apart from the ordinary "chivalric" acts of men in the detail of social life. This question of sex, therefore, as before said, forms the solitary exception to the general law of the *esprit de corps* of those possessing common characteristics and interests. It cannot be adequately explained by a reference to the evolution of sex functions and relations from primitive man onwards, since it is at least in the extreme form we see it to-day, a comparatively recent social phenomenon. The theory of the sacrosanctity of women by virtue of their sex, quite apart from their character and conduct as individuals, scarcely dates back farther than a century, even from its beginnings. The earlier chivalry, where it obtained at all, applied only to the woman who presented what were conceived of as the ideal moral feminine characteristics in some appreciable degree. The mere physical fact of sex was never for a moment regarded as of itself sufficient to entitle the woman to any special homage, consideration, or immunity, over and above the man. No one suggested that the female criminal was less guilty or more excusable than the male criminal. No one believed that a woman had a vested right to rob or swindle a man because she had had sexual relations with him. This notion of the mere fact of sex—of femality—as of itself constituting a title to special privileges and immunities, apart from any other consideration, is a product of very recent times. In treating this question, in so far as it bears on the criminal law, it is important to distinguish carefully between the softening of the whole system of punishment due to the general development of humanitarian tendencies and the special discrimination made in favour of the female sex. These two things are very often inadequately distinguished from one another. Punishment may have become more humane where men are concerned, it may have advanced up to a certain point in this direction, but its character is not essentially changed. As regards women, however, the whole conception of criminal punishment and penal discipline has altered. Sex privilege has been now definitely established as a principle.

Now a complete investigation of the psychology of this curious phenomenon we have been considering—namely, the hatred so common with men for their fellow-men as a sex—is a task which has never yet been properly taken in hand. Its obverse side is to be seen on all hands in the conferring and confirming of sex prerogative on women. Not very long ago, as we have seen, one of its most striking manifestations came strongly under public notice—namely, the "rule of the sea," by which women, by virtue of their sex, can claim to be saved from a sinking ship before men. The fact that the laws and practices in which this man-hatred and woman-preference find expression are contrary to every elementary sense of justice, in many cases conflict with public policy, and can obviously be seen to be purely arbitrary, matters not. The majority of men feel no *sense* of the injustice although they may admit the fact of the injustice, when categorically questioned. They are prepared when it comes to the point to let public policy go by the board rather than entrench upon the sacred privilege and immunity of the female; while as to the arbitrary and unreasoning nature of the aforesaid laws and practices, not being troubled with a logical conscience, this does not affect them. I must confess to being unequal to the task of accurately fathoming the psychological condition of the average man who hates man in general and loves woman in general to the extent of going contrary to so many apparently basal tendencies of human nature as we know it otherwise. The reply, of course, will be an appeal to the power of the sexual instinct. But this, I must again repeat, will not explain the rise, or, if not the rise, at least the marked expansion of the sentiment in question during the last three generations or thereabouts. Even apart from this, while I am well aware of the power of sexual love to effect anything in the mind of man as regards its individual object, I submit it is difficult to conceive how it can influence so strongly men's attitude towards women they have not seen, or, even where they have seen them, when there is no question of sexual attraction, or, again, as regards the collectivity of women—the abstract category, Woman (in general).

We have already dealt with the Anti-man campaign in the Press, especially in modern novels and plays. This, as we have remarked, often takes the form of direct abuse of husbands and lovers and the attempt to make them look ridiculous as a foil to the brilliant qualities of wives and sweethearts. But we sometimes find the mere laudation of woman herself, apart from any direct anti-manism, assume the character of an intellectual emetic. A much-admired contemporary novelist, depicting a wedding ceremony in fashionable society circles, describes the feelings of his hero, a young man disgusted with the hollowness and vanity of "Society" and all its ways, as follows:—"The bride was opposite him now, and by an instinct of common chivalry he turned away his eyes; it seemed to him a shame to look at that downcast head above the silver mystery of her perfect raiment; the modest head full, doubtless, of devotion and pure yearnings; the stately head where no such thought as 'How am I looking this day of all days, before all London?' had ever entered: the proud head, where no such fear as, 'How am I carrying it off?' could surely be besmirching. . . . He saw below the surface of this drama played before his eyes; and set his face, as a man might who found himself assisting at a sacrifice." Now, I ask, can it be believed that the writer of the above flamboyant feminist fustian is a novelist and playwright of established reputation who undoubtedly has done good work. The obvious criticism must surely strike every reader that it is somewhat strange that this divinely innocent creature he glorifies should arise straight out of a _milieu_ which is shown up as the embodiment of hollowness and conventional superficiality. If men can lay the butter on thick in their laudation of womanhood, female idolaters of their own sex can fairly outbid them. At the time of writing there has just come under my notice a dithyramb in the journal, _The Clarion_, by Miss Winnifred Blatchford, on the sacrosanct perfections of womanhood in general, especially as exemplified in the suicidal exploits of the late lamented Emily Wilding Davidson of Epsom fame, and a diatribe on the purity, beauty and unapproachable glory of woman. According to this lady, the glory of womanhood seems to extend to every part of the female organism, but, we are told, is especially manifested in the hair (oozing into the roots apparently). Evidently there is something especially sacred in woman's hair! This prose ode to Woman, as exemplified in Emily Davidson, culminates in the invocation: "Will the day ever come when a woman's life will be rated higher . . . than that of a jockey?" Poor jockey! We will trust not, though present appearances do indicate a strong tendency to regard a woman as possessing the prerogatives of the sacred cow of Indian or ancient Egyptian fame!

It is impossible to read or hear any discussion on, say, the marriage laws, without it being apparent that the female side of the question is the one element of the problem which is considered worthy of attention. The undoubted iniquity of our existing marriage laws is always spoken of as an injustice to the woman and the changes in the direction of greater freedom which are advocated as a relief to the wife bound to a bad or otherwise unendurable husband. That the converse case may happen, that that reviled and despised thing, a husband, may also have reason to desire relief from a wife whose angelic qualities and vast superiority to his own vile male self he fails to appreciate, never seems to enter into the calculation at all.

That no satisfactory formulation of the psychology of the movement of Feminism has yet been offered is undoubtedly true. For the moment, I take it, all we can do is co-ordinate the fact as a case of what we may term social hypnotism, of those waves of feeling uninfluenced by reason which are a phenomenon so common in history—witchcraft manias, flagellant fanaticisms, religious "revivals," and similar social upheavals. The belief that woman is oppressed by man, and that the need for remedying that oppression at all costs is urgent, partly, at least, doubtless belongs to this order of phenomena. That this feeling is widespread and held in various degrees of intensity by large numbers of persons, men no less than women, is not to be denied. That it is of the nature of a hypnotic wave of sentiment, uninfluenced by reason, is shown by the fact that argument does not seem to touch it. You may show conclusively that facts are opposed to the assumption; that, so far from women being oppressed, the very contrary is the case; that the existing law and its administration is in no essential respect whatever unfavourable to women, but, on the contrary, is, as a whole, grossly unfair to men—it is all to no purpose. Your remonstrances, in the main, fall on deaf ears, or, shall we say, they fall off the mind coated with Feminist sentiment as water falls from the proverbial duck's back. The facts are ignored and the sentiment prevails; the same old catchwords, the same lies and threadbare fallacies are repeated. The fact that they have been shown to be false counts for nothing. The hypnotic wave of sentiment sweeps reason aside and compels men to believe that woman is oppressed and man the oppressor, and believe it they will. If facts are against the *idée fixe* of the hypnotic suggestion, so much the worse for the facts. Thus far the Feminist dogma of the oppression of the female sex.

As regards the obverse side of this Sentimental Feminism which issues in ferocious sex-laws directed against men for offences against women—laws enacting barbarous tortures, such as the "cat," and which are ordered with gusto in all their severity in our criminal courts—this probably is largely traceable to the influence of Sadic lusts. An agitation such as that which led to the passing of the White Slave Traffic Act, so-called, of 1912, is started, an agitation engineered largely by the inverted libidinousness of social purity mongers, and on the crest of this agitation the votaries of Sadic cruelty have their innings. The foolish Sentimental Feminist at large, whose indignation against wicked man is fanned to fury by bogus tales and his judgment captured by representations of the severities requisite to stamp out the evil he is assured is so widespread, lends his fatuous support to the measures proposed. The judicial Bench is, of course, delighted at the increase of power given it over the prisoner in the dock, and should any of the *puisnes* happen to have Sadic proclivities they are as happy as horses in clover and the "cat" flourishes like a green bay tree.

Let us now turn to the question of the psychology of Political Feminism. Political Feminism, as regards its immediate demand of female suffrage, is based directly on the modern conception of democracy. This is its avowed basis. With modern notions of universal suffrage it is declared that the exclusion of women from the franchise is logically incompatible. If you include in the parliamentary voting lists all sorts and conditions of men, it is said, it is plainly a violation of the principle of democracy to exclude more than one half of the adult population from the polls. As Mill used to say in his advocacy of female suffrage, so long as the franchise was restricted to a very small section of the population, there may have been nothing noteworthy in the exclusion of women. But now that the mass of men are entitled to the vote and the avowed aim of democracy is to extend it to all men, the refusal to extend it still further to women is an anomaly and a manifest inconsistency. But in this, Mill, and others who have used his argument, omitted to consider one very vital point. The extensions of the suffrage, such as have been demanded and in part obtained by democracy up to the present agitation, have always referred to the removal of class barriers, wealth barriers, race barriers, etc.—in a word, social barriers—but never to the removal of barriers based on deep-lying organic difference—*i.e.* barriers determining not sociological but biological distinctions. The case of sex is unique in this connection, and this fact vitiates any analogy between the extension of suffrage to women and its extension to fresh social strata such as democracy has hitherto had in view, terminating in the manhood suffrage which is the ultimate goal of all political democrats. Now sex constitutes an organic or biological difference, just as a species constitutes another and (of course) a stronger biological difference. Hence I contend the mere fact of this difference rules out the bare appeal to the principle of democracy *per se* as an argument in favour of the extension of the suffrage to women. There is, I submit, no parity between the principle and practice of democracy as hitherto understood, and the new extension proposed to be given to the franchise by the inclusion of women within its pale. And yet there is no question but that the apparent but delusive demand of logical consistency in this question, has influenced and still influences many an honest democrat in his attitude in this matter.

But although the recognition of the difference of sex as being an organic difference and therefore radically other than social differences of caste, class, wealth, or even race, undoubtedly invalidates the appeal to the democrat on the ground of consistency, to accept the principle of female suffrage, yet it does not necessarily dispose of the question. It merely leaves the ground free for the problem as to whether the organic distinction implied in sex does or does not involve corresponding intellectual and moral differences in the female sex which it is proposed to enfranchise; and furthermore whether such differences, if they exist, involve general inferiority, or at least an unfitness *ad hoc* for the exercise of political functions. These questions we have, I think, sufficiently discussed already in the present work. The fact of the existence of exceptionally able women in various departments, does undoubtedly mislead many men in their judgment as to the capacity of the average woman to "think politically," or otherwise to show herself the effective equal of the average man, morally and intellectually. The reasons for answering this question in the negative we have already briefly indicated in the course of our investigations. This renders it unnecessary to discuss the matter any further here.

In dealing with the psychological aspects of the Feminist Movement, the intellectual conditions which paved the way for its acceptance, it is worth while recalling two or three typical instances of the class of "argument" to be heard on occasion from the female advocates for the suffrage. Thus, when the census was taken in 1911 and the Women's Political and Social Union conceived, as they thought, the brilliant idea of annoying the authorities and vitiating the results of the census by refusing to allow themselves to be enrolled, one of the leaders, when interviewed on the point, gave her reason for her refusal to be included, in the following terms: —"I am not a citizen" (meaning that she did not possess the franchise) "and I am not going to pretend to be one." The silliness of this observation is, of course, obvious, seeing that the franchise or even citizenship has nothing whatever to do with the census, which includes infants, besides criminals, lunatics, imbeciles, etc. Again, in a manifesto of the Women's Political and Social Union defending window-smashing and other "militant" outrages, it was pointed out that the coal strike had caused more injury than the window-smashing and yet the strikers were not prosecuted as the window-smashers were—in other words, the exercise of the basal personal right of the free man to withhold his labour save under the conditions agreed to by him, is paralleled with criminal outrage against person and property! Again, some three or four years ago, when the Women's Suffrage Bill had passed the Commons, on its being announced by the Government that for the remainder of the Session no further facilities could be given for private members' Bills, save for those of a non-contentious character, one of these sapient females urged in the Press that, seeing that there were persons to be found in both the orthodox political camps who were in favour of female suffrage, therefore the Bill in question must be regarded as of a non-contentious character! Once more, a lady, writing a few months ago to one of the weekly journals, remarked that though deliberate window-breaking, destruction of letters, and arson, might be illegal acts, yet that the punishing of them by imprisonment with hard labour, they being political offences, was also an illegal act, with the conclusion that the "militants" and the authorities, both alike having committed illegal acts, were "quits"! These choice specimens of suffragettes' logic are given as throwing a significant light on the mental condition of women in the suffragette movement, and indirectly on female psychology generally. One would presumably suppose that the women who put them forward must have failed to see the exhibition they were making of themselves. That any human being out of an asylum, could have sunk to the depth of fatuous inconsequent idiocy they indicate would seem scarcely credible. Is the order of imbecility which the above and many similar utterances reflect, confined to suffragette intelligence alone, or does it point to radical inferiority of intellectual fibre, not in degree merely, but in kind, in the mental constitution of the human female generally? Certainly it is hard to think that any man, however low his intelligence, would be capable of making a fool of himself precisely in the way these women are continually doing in their attempts to defend their cause and their tactics.

In the foregoing pages we have endeavoured to trace some of the leading strands of thought going to make up the Modern Feminist Movement. Sentimental Feminism clearly has its roots in sexual feeling, and in the tradition of chivalry, albeit the notion of chivalry has essentially changed in the course of its evolution. For the rest, Sentimental Feminism, with its double character of man-antipathy and woman-sympathy, as we see it to-day, has assumed the character of one of those psychopathic social phenomena which have so often recurred in history. It can only be explained, like the latter, as an hypnotic wave passing over society.

As for Political Feminism, we have shown that this largely has its root in a fallacious application of the notion of democracy, partaking largely of the logical fallacy known technically as *a dicto secundum quid ad dictum simpliciter*. This logical fallacy of Political Feminism is, of course, reinforced and urged forward by Sentimental Feminism. As coming under the head of the psychology of the movement, we have also called attention to some curious phenomena of logical imbecility, noticeable in the utterances of educated women in the suffragette agitation.

CHAPTER VIII

THE INDICTMENT

Feminism, or, as it is sometimes called, the emancipation of woman, as we know it in the present day, may be justifiably indicted as a gigantic fraud —a fraud in its general aim and a fraud alike in its methods of controversy and in its practical tactics. It is through and through disingenuous and dishonest. Modern Feminism has always professed to be a movement for political and social equality between the sexes. The claim for this equalising of position and rights in modern society is logically based upon the assumption of an essential equality in natural ability between the sexes. As to this, we have indicated in the preceding pages on broad lines, the grounds for regarding the foregoing assumption as false. But quite apart from this question, I contend the fraudulent nature of the present movement can readily be seen by showing it to be not merely based on false grounds, but directly and consciously fraudulent in its pretensions.

It uniformly professes to aim at the placing of the sexes on a footing of social and political equality. A very little inquiry into its concrete demands suffices to show that its aim, so far from being equality, is the very reverse —viz. to bring about, with the aid of men themselves, as embodied in the forces of the State, a female ascendancy and a consolidation and extension of already existing female privileges. That this is so may be seen in general by the constant conjunction of Political and Sentimental Feminism in the same persons. It may be seen more particularly in detail, in the specific demands of Feminists. These demands, as formulated by suffragists as a reason why the vote is essential to the interests of women, amount to little if anything else than proposals for laws to enslave and browbeat men and to admit women to virtual if not actual immunity for all offences committed against men. It is enough to consult any suggestions for a woman's "charter" in order to confirm what is here said. Such proposals invariably suggest the sacrificing of man at every turn to woman.[162:1]

> [162:1] This is arrived at by the clever trick of appealing to the modern theory of the equal mental capacity of the sexes when it is a question of political and economic rights and advantages for women, and of counterappealing to the

traditional sentiment based on the belief in the inferiority of the female sex, when it is a question of legal and administrative privilege and consideration. The Feminist thus succeeds by his dexterity in the usually difficult feat of "getting it both ways" for his fair clients.

In the early eighties of the last century appeared a skit in the form of a novel from the pen of the late Sir Walter Besant, entitled "The Revolt of Man," depicting the oppression of man under a Feminist régime, an oppression which ended in a revolt and the re-establishment of male supremacy. The ideas underlying this *jeu d'esprit* of the subjection of men would seem to be seriously entertained by the female leaders of the present woman's movement. It is many years ago now since a minister holding one of the highest positions in the present Cabinet made the remark to me: —"The real object, you know, for which these women want the vote is simply to get rascally laws passed against men!" Subsequent Feminist agitation has abundantly proved the truth of this observation. An illustration of the practical results of the modern woman's movement is to be seen in the infamous White Slave Traffic Act of 1912 rushed through Parliament as a piece of panic legislation by dint of a campaign of sheer hard lying. The atrocity of this act has been sufficiently dealt with in a previous chapter. [163:1]

> [163:1] There is one fortunate thing as regards these savage laws aimed at the suppression of certain crimes, and that is, as it would seem, they are never effective in achieving their purpose. As Mr Tighe Hopkins remarks, apropos of the torture of the "cat" ("Wards of the State," p. 203):—"The attempt to correct crime with crime has everywhere repaid us in the old properly disastrous way." It would indeed be regrettable if it could be shown that penal laws of this kind were successful. Far better is it that the crimes of isolated individuals should continue than that crimes such as the cold-blooded infliction of torture and death committed at the behest of the State, as supposed to represent the whole of society, should attain their object, even though the object be the suppression of crimes of another kind perpetrated by the aforesaid individuals within society. The successful repression of crimes committed by individuals, by a crime committed by State authority, can only act as an encouragement to the State to continue its course of inflicting punishment which is itself a crime.

Other results of the inequality between the sexes so effectively urged by present-day Feminism, may be seen in the conduct of magistrates, judges and juries, in our courts civil and criminal. This has been already animadverted upon in the course of the present work, and illustrative cases given, as also in previous writings of the present author to which allusion has already been made. It is not too much to say that a man has practically no chance in the present day in a court of law, civil or criminal, of obtaining justice where a woman is in the case. The savage vindictiveness exhibited towards men, as displayed in the eagerness of judges to obtain, and the readiness of juries to return, convictions against men accused of crimes against women, on evidence which, in many cases, would not be good enough (to use the common phrase) to hang a dog on, with the inevitable ferocious sentence following conviction, may be witnessed on almost every occasion when such cases are up for trial. I have spoken of the eagerness of judges to obtain convictions. As an illustration of this sort of thing, the following may be given:—In the trial of a man for the murder of a woman, before Mr Justice Bucknill, which took place some time ago, it came out in evidence that the woman had violently and obscenely abused and threatened the man immediately before, in the presence of other persons. The jury were so impressed with the evidence of unusually strong provocation that they hesitated whether it was not sufficient to reduce the crime to that of manslaughter, and, unable to agree offhand on a verdict of murder, asked the judge for further guidance. Their deliberations were, however, cut short by the judge, who remarked on the hesitation they had in arriving at their verdict, finally adding: "Only think, gentlemen, how you would view it had this been your own wife or sister who was cruelly done to death!" With the habitual obsequiousness of a British jury towards the occupant of the Bench, the gentlemen in question swallowed complacently the insult thrown at their wives and sisters in putting them in the same category with a foul strumpet, and promptly did what the judge obviously wanted of them—to wit, brought in a verdict of wilful murder. The cases on the obverse side, where the judge, by similar sentimental appeal, aims at procuring the acquittal of female prisoners notoriously guilty on the evidence, that palladium of rogues, the English law of libel, precludes me from referring to individually. As regards the disparity in punishment, however, we have an apt and recent illustration in the execution of the youth of nineteen, convicted on doubtful evidence of the murder of his sweetheart, and the reprieve of the woman convicted on her own admission of the murder of her paramour by soaking him in paraffin during his sleep and setting him alight!

Another effect of the influence of Sentimental Feminism, is seen in crimes of the "unwritten law" description, the *crime passionel* of the

French. The most atrocious and dastardly murders and other crimes of violence are condoned and even glorified if they can but be covered by the excuse that they are dictated by a desire to avenge a woman's "honour" or to enable her to obtain the object of her wishes. The incident in Sir J. M. Barrie's play of the lady who murders a man by throwing him out of a railway carriage over a dispute respecting the opening of a window, and gets acquitted on the excuse that her little girl had got a cold, represents a not exaggerated picture of "modern justice"—for women only! The outrageous application of the principles, if such you may call them, of Sentimental Feminism in this country in the case of the suffragettes, has made English justice and penal administration the laughing-stock of the world. But the way in which the crimes of the suffragettes have been dealt with, is after all only a slight exaggeration of the immunity from all the severer penalties of the law enjoyed by female convicts generally. This has been carried in the case of suffragette criminals to the utmost limits of absurdity. In fact, the deference exhibited towards these deliberate perpetrators of crimes of wanton destruction is sometimes comic, as in the case of the Richmond magistrate who rebuked the policeman-witness in an arson charge for omitting the "Miss" in referring to one of the female prisoners in the dock: as well as in the "high character" usually attributed to the perpetrators of these deeds of outrage and violence even by certain functionaries of Church and State. They did not speak in this strain morebetoken, when mere male anarchists or Fenians were involved in difficulties with the law due to overzeal for their cause!

The whole movement, it is quite evident, depends for its success, largely, at least, on the apathy of men. The bulk of men undoubtedly do not sympathise with the pretensions of the Feminist agitation, but the bulk of men are indifferent one way or the other. They do not take the Feminist Movement seriously. The bare notion of women, as such, being a danger to men as such, strikes them as absurd. They do not realise that the question is not of the physical strength of women as women, but of the whole forces of the State being at the disposal of women to set in motion to gratify their whims and passions. The idea of a sex war in which women take the field against men, such as represents the inwardness of the whole Feminist Movement of to-day, seems to them ridiculous. The feeling at the root of most men's good-humoured patronage of, or indifference to, Modern

Feminist claims, is roughly expressed in a remark of the late William Morris in replying to some animadversions of mine on the subject:—"What does it matter? A man ought to be always able to deal with a woman if necessary. Why, I could tackle a half dozen women at once for that matter!" This is a common attitude of mind on the subject among otherwise sane and sensible men. The absurdity of it is manifest when one considers that the issue of man versus woman as units of physical strength respectively, is purely irrelevant. It is not a question of the man tackling the woman or any number of women. It is the question of the whole force of the State tackling the man *in favour* of the woman. The prevalent idea in many men's minds seems to be that of the State drawing a ring-fence around the disputant man and woman and letting them fight the matter out between themselves, which, to speak the language of the great geometer of antiquity—"is absurd."

Modern Feminism, tacking itself on to an older tradition which it travesties beyond all recognition, has succeeded in affecting modern public opinion with an overpowering sense of the sacrosanctity of human femality as such. It is not content with respect for the ideal of *good* womanhood but it would fain place on a pedestal the mere fact of femalehood in itself. This is illustrated in a thousand ways. Thus while public opinion tolerates the most bestial and infamous forms of corporal punishment for men in gaols, it will regard the slight chastisement by the medical head of an institution for mental cases, of a girl who is admittedly obstinate and refractory rather than mentally afflicted in the ordinary sense of the term, as "degrading."

Again, in order to sustain its favourite thesis, the intellectual equality of woman with man, it resorts, whenever a plausible case presents itself, to its usual policy of the falsification of fact. Take the instance of Madame Curie. When radium was first discovered in the laboratory of the late Professor Curie we were told that the latter had made the discovery, it being at the same time mentioned that he possessed in his wife a valuable aid in his laboratory work. We were afterwards told that the discovery of radium was the joint work of both, the implication being that the honours were equally divided. Now, Feminist influence has succeeded in getting Madame Curie spoken of as herself the discoverer of radium! I venture to affirm that there is no evidence whatever for assuming that radium would ever have seen the light had the late Professor Curie not himself experimented in his laboratory, not to speak of his predecessor Becquerel.

We have seen that Feminists are, in this country, at least, zealous in championing the Puritan view of sexual morality. Many of them, in the vehemence of their Anti-man crusade, look forward with relish to the opportunity they anticipate will be afforded them when women get the vote, of passing laws rigorously enforcing asceticism on men by means of severe penal enactments. All forms of indulgence (by men), sexual or otherwise, uncongenial to the puritanic mind, would be equally placed under the ban of the criminal law! Anyone desirous of testing the truth of the above statement has only to read the suffragette papers and other expositions of the gospel of Feminism as held by its most devoted advocates.

One point should not be lost sight of, and that is the attitude of the Press. Almost all journals are ready to publish any argument in favour of the suffrage or of the other claims of the movement on behalf of women. In defiance of this fact, a prominent Feminist prelate some time ago, in a letter to *The Times*, alleged among the other so-called grievances of women at the present day, and apparently as in some sort a condonation of "militancy," that the Press was closed to women anxious to air their grievances! A statement more directly the reverse of the truth could hardly have been made. Open any paper of general circulation—say any of the morning dailies—and you will find letters galore advocating the Feminist side of the question! According to my own observation, they are in the proportion of something like three or four in favour to one against. The fact is useless denying that this sex-agitation has every favour shown it by current "public opinion," including even that of its opponents. Female "militants" of the suffrage have pleas urged in condonation of their criminal acts, such as their alleged "high character," which would be laughed at in the case of men— and yet they whine at being boycotted.

The readiness, and almost eagerness, with which certain sections of British public opinion are ready to view favourably anything urged on behalf of female suffrage, is aptly illustrated by the well-known argument we so often hear when the existence of "militancy" is pointed out as a reason for withholding the suffrage—the argument, namely, as to the unfairness of refusing the franchise to numbers of peaceable and law-abiding women who are asking for it, because a relatively small section of women resort to criminal methods of emphasising their demand. Now let us examine the real interpretation of the facts. It is quite true that the majority of the women agitating for the suffrage at the present day are themselves non-militants. But what is and has been their attitude towards their militant sisters? Have they ever repudiated the criminal tactics of the latter with the decision and even indignation one might reasonably have expected had they really regarded the campaign of violence and wanton outrage with strong disapprobation, not to say abhorrence? The answer must be a decided negative. At the very most they mildly rebuke the unwisdom of militant methods, blessing them, as it were, with faint blame, while, as a general rule, they will not go even so far as this, but are content, while graciously deigning to tell you that, although their own methods are not those of militancy, yet that they and the militants are alike working for the same end, notwithstanding they may differ as to the most effective methods of attaining it. The non-militant woman suffragist is always careful never to appear an *anti*-militant. Everyone can see that had the bulk of the so-called "peaceable and law-abiding" suffragists, to whose claims we are enjoined to give ear, honestly and resolutely set their faces against, and vigorously denounced, the criminal campaign, refusing to have anything to do with it or its authors, the campaign in question would have come to an end long ago. But no! this would not have suited the book of the "peaceable and law-abiding" advocates of woman's suffrage. Their aim has been, and is still, to run with the "militant" hare and hunt with the "peaceable and law-abiding" hounds. While themselves abstaining from any unlawful act they are perfectly willing and desirous that they and their movement shall reap all the advantages of advertisement and otherwise that may accrue from the militant policy. That the above is a true state of the case as regards the "peaceful and law-abiding" elements in the suffragist movement, which we are assured so largely outnumber the militant section, one would think must be plain to everyone, however obtuse, who has followed with attention the course of the present agitation. And yet there are fools of the male sex who consider seriously this preposterous plea of the injustice of refusing to concede the suffrage to a large number of "peaceable and law-abiding" women who are demanding it, because of the action of a small body of violent females—with whom, *bien entendu,* the aforesaid large body of "peaceable and law-abiding" women (while keeping themselves carefully aloof from active participation in militancy), do not pretend to conceal their sympathy!

The whole modern woman's movement is based, in a measure, at least, on an assumption which is absolutely unfounded—to wit, that man has systematically oppressed woman in the past, that the natural tendency of evil-minded man is always to oppress woman, or, to put it from the other side, that woman is the victim of man's egoism! The unsoundness of this view ought to be apparent to every unbiassed student of history, anthropology, and physiology. The Feminist prefers to see evidence of male oppression in the place woman has occupied in social and political life, rather than the natural consequence of her organic constitution, her secondary sexual characteristics, and the natural average inferiority which flows therefrom. As regards the personal relations between men and women, an impartial view of the case must inevitably lead to the conclusion that whatever else man in general may have on his conscience, no reasonable reproach lies to his score as regards his treatment of woman. The patience, forbearance, and kindliness, with which, from Socrates downwards, men as a rule have encountered the whims, the tempers, and the tantrums of their often unworthy womankind is indeed a marvel. But it is a still greater marvel that Modern Feminism in this, as in other things, should have succeeded in hocussing public opinion into the delusion that the exact opposite of the truth represents the real state of the case. This, however, is a marvel which runs through the history of the controversial exploits of the whole Feminist Movement.

In the foregoing pages we have striven to unmask the shameless imposture which, in the main, this movement represents. We have tracked down one dishonest argument after another. We have pointed out how the thinnest and hollowest of subterfuges are allowed to pass muster, and even to become current coin, by dint of unrefuted reiteration. The Feminist trick of reversing the facts of the case, as, for example, the assertion that man-made law and its administration is unjust to women, and then raising a howl of indignation at the position of affairs they picture, such being, of course, the diametrical opposite of the real facts—all this has been exposed. In conclusion I can only express the hope that honest, straightforward men who have been bitten by Feminist wiles will take pause and reconsider their position. Whatever sentiment or sympathy they may have with the aims of the movement intrinsically, it ought to be not too much to expect them to view with contempt and abhorrence the mass of disingenuous falsehood and transparent subterfuge, which the votaries of Feminism systematically seek to palm off upon a public opinion—only too easily gullible in this matter—as true fact and valid argument.